The Seven-Figure Practice Blueprint for Dentists

BEN FRIBERG, DDS

THE SEVEN FIGURE PRACTICE BLUEPRINT

FOR DENTISTS

HOW TO LEAD, MANAGE, AND MARKET A FULFILLING PRACTICE

FRIBERG ADVISORS
WILMINGTON, NORTH CAROLINA

Friberg Advisors
Wilmington, North Carolina

Copyright © 2025 by Ben Friberg. All rights reserved.

LCCN: 2025908933

Paperback ISBN: 979-8-9925874-0-1
eBook ISBN: 979-8-9925874-1-8

All rights reserved. No part of this publication may be reproduced, stored in a retrieval system or transmitted in any form or by any means (electronic, mechanical, photocopying, recording, or otherwise) without the written permission of the author and publisher.

Book cover and interior design by Faceout Studio
Editorial production by KN Literary Arts

drbenfriberg.com

To the dentists who have dedicated their lives to transforming smiles and improving the health and confidence of their patients—this book is for you.

Your unwavering commitment to excellence, your resilience in the face of challenges, and your passion for serving others inspire us all. May this book serve as a guide to help you not only achieve the thriving practice of your dreams but also find joy and fulfillment in the journey.

*Thank you for the work you do.
It truly changes lives.
I hope this book helps change yours.*

CONTENTS

Foreword 9

Introduction 11

PART I: LEADERSHIP

1. Drafting Your Blueprint 21
2. Making Your Life Concrete 39
3. Permission Granted 59
4. Team Culture 93

PART II: MANAGEMENT

5. When to Lead and What to Manage 123
6. Business Systems 149
7. Metrics and KPIs 171

PART III: MARKETING

8. You Are the CMO 193
9. Internal and External Marketing 217
10. Philanthropy 251

Conclusion 267
Endnotes 271
Acknowledgments 273

FOREWORD

by Dr. Kyle Stanley
Founder, Light Side Academy

Dentistry is an incredible profession—one that combines artistry, science, and the ability to change lives every single day. But it's also a career that can take an enormous toll on us, not just physically, but mentally and emotionally. Too many dentists find themselves trapped in a cycle of stress, burnout, and disillusionment, wondering why their dream career feels like a burden.

I've lived this reality. As dentists, we are trained to master clinical skills, but we are never truly prepared for the mental weight of running a practice, leading a team, and managing the expectations of both patients and ourselves. Over time, the pressure can rob us of the very passion that brought us into this field. That's why I've dedicated my career to helping dental professionals master their mental and relational health—because success isn't just about production numbers or a seven-figure practice; it's about building a career that sustains you, rather than one that consumes you.

This book is different. It doesn't just focus on the tactical aspects of growing a profitable practice; it lays the foundation for a fulfilling and sustainable career. *The Seven-Figure Practice Blueprint for Dentists* provides a clear path to leadership, management, and marketing—key pillars allowing you to control your practice rather than letting it control you. More importantly, it helps you redefine success on your terms, ensuring that your career aligns with your values, vision, and overall well-being.

Benjamin Friberg has done an outstanding job distilling years of experience into actionable strategies that any dentist can implement. His insights will challenge the way you think about your practice, your leadership, and, most importantly, your life.

For any dentist who feels overwhelmed, overworked, or on the verge of burnout—this book is your wake-up call. It's time to take back control. It's time to build a thriving practice that works for you, not against you.

Let's get to work.

INTRODUCTION

Getting home from work at 8:45 p.m. isn't great, especially when you saw your first patient more than 12 hours prior. Yet for too many years, this was my life: long days working my dreaded schedule of 8:00 a.m. to 8:00 p.m., listening to a podcast on "dental whatever" on my 35-minute commute home, and rushing inside with the hope of kissing my kids goodnight—even though deep down, I knew it would be another missed bedtime. How many more would I miss before there weren't any left?

I'd crack a beer as my reward for a hard day, or a good day, or a long day—just because that's what I did after work. No real benefit; just slow consequences. I'd mumble something to my wife about how my day went as we sat, staring at the glowing box in the living room. Just going through the motions. Another beer, another episode—and maybe another beer because I didn't want to go to sleep quite yet. Going to sleep meant I'd be that much closer to driving back to the office I'd just left. No break, no rest, and certainly not what I had dreamed about when I first opened my practice.

I can still remember the Tuesday morning huddle three years after we opened when it finally hit me. As I looked around the room, it was like someone had taken the blinders off. The excitement was gone. My staff was exhausted. All eight of us were staring at the floor, trying to muster up the courage to create an "amazing five-star patient experience" with only one-star energy. I realized in that moment that it didn't have to be that way. It wasn't supposed to be like this, and I was going to do something about it. So I did.

Fast-forward three years later and I'm standing on a cliff face, strapped into a cable, traversing a *via ferrata* in one of the most beautiful places in the world: Lauterbrunnen, Switzerland. It's just after sunrise and I'm on a twelve-day vacation with my family, checking off bucket-list items for each of us while my team is doing the same all across the world. This is just one of many vacations I take every year—each to amazing destinations, and each with bucket-list items being crossed off. I now take seven weeks off annually, work twenty-seven hours clinically per week, and get to eat dinner with my family every night. I'm in the best shape of my life. I work Monday through Thursday, only seeing large specialty cases on Fridays. And throughout all those changes, we've seen an increase in profitability, a reduction in production, and a renewed passion for creating the best experience for every patient. The practice will close out the year with over $2,000,000 in production and averaging over 45 new patients per month. We hit industry-standard KPIs and received over 300 five-star reviews for the year.

This is what my vision for my life was when I made that fateful decision to become a dentist. But like so many of my colleagues, I found that the path to achieve this was a rocky one. The changes required to get to this point came through working with close friends and experts inside and outside the dental field. It involved an intentional remapping of my life, my leadership skills, my management, and my practice marketing to literally reinvent my business into what I actually dreamed of when I chose to be a dentist.

This book is about that transformation. I know where you are and I can help you. By choosing to become a dentist, you have opened yourself up to endless possibilities. Whether you want to climb mountains in Switzerland, spend more time with your family, or retire early, dentistry can provide all those things. But it can also run your life like it did mine if you're not careful. This is a trap that far too many dentists fall into, and one that I am personally committed to helping you avoid. So if that sounds intriguing, I'd recommend you keep reading.

My Story

My path to this point is different from most doctors. I started in the business world when I was nineteen years old. I'd wanted to be a general contractor, so I pursued a management degree with a minor in construction engineering. I joined an internship program to help pay for college and learn how to run my own business—an internship which happened to involve running a division of a painting company for an organization called College Works Painting. Yes, you read that right: I ran a painting company at the age of 19. It was as crazy as it sounds. I was responsible for sales and marketing, hiring, inventory management, production management, scheduling, and equipment. As you can imagine, this was a trial-by-fire experience where I learned many of the elements of running a business. In just under six months, I launched a business, built a team of 10 employees, and became one of the top managers nationwide, out of more than 1,000 branches.

From there, I was promoted to the position of district manager for the state of Oregon and maintained a top-five status in the nation. As a district manager, I had the opportunity to conduct over 1,000 interviews per year and run weekend training seminars for over 100 new employees. I worked at an executive level of this multimillion-dollar painting company that operated with an average employee age of twenty years old. It was leadership training under fire, and I loved it. I was able to help hundreds of college students learn business principles, motivate them to give up their evenings and weekends to knock on doors instead of partying, and manage the expectations of homeowners when things didn't go well—and believe me, sometimes they didn't.

After graduating with my business management degree and a minor in construction engineering, I was recruited to open two divisions of a commercial restoration company. This company grew quickly, and within three years had over 100 employees and several million in revenue. At twenty-three years old, I was sitting in boardrooms with seasoned investors and property managers, trying to convince them that they should trust me with six-figure projects when I could barely use a paintbrush myself. It was a huge learning experience that I'm now incredibly grateful for.

On the outside, everything looked great. I'd excelled quickly in my career and was performing at a much higher level than my peers. But I was riddled with anxiety and didn't enjoy what I was doing. I didn't feel like I had meaningful relationships with anybody. The work I was doing didn't have a lasting impact. There were a lot of things I needed in order to be satisfied in my life that weren't there because, ultimately, it wasn't just about making a bunch of money for me. I wasn't spending significant time with my family. We had dreams of traveling, but we weren't actually doing it. Even if we went on a weekend trip, I was so burnt out from work that I wasn't present. Those trips were actually more stressful than relaxing because I constantly felt like I needed to be back at the office.

Now, I can look back on that time and see how important it was to my success today. But I'm not going to sugarcoat it: That was an incredibly difficult time. My drive and ambition were outrunning my emotional maturity to the point where, one day, I found myself alone in the woods with a gun, contemplating suicide. Through years of counseling and the use of medication, I was able to overcome those challenging thoughts and feelings.

During the 2008 financial crisis, my partners and I decided to close the northwest division of the company. My wife, Ella, who'd been with me since I started the company, was incredibly supportive during this time—a trend that would continue throughout this long, complicated journey. I was relieved—elated, even—to be free of a business that I wasn't happy in. I went from being stressed, tired, and worn down back to my normal self—even though I was unemployed during one of the largest recessions in modern history. It was at this point that I decided to pursue healthcare.

So I went back to school to be a physical therapist. I'd wrestled all the way into college as a high school state champion, and I'd been in physical therapy through much of that time for obvious reasons.

I thought I could relate well to athletes and people who'd been injured in that recovery process.

But my mother-in-law is actually a dentist herself, and she slowly convinced me that dentistry was the way to go instead of physical therapy. I ended up volunteering on an international medical team RV that drove around to different homeless encampments or church organizations that worked with people in need, offering free dentistry. When I volunteered on that bus, I fell in love with the practice. The joy that I saw in people's faces and the intense gratitude they expressed after getting their dental work done—I knew that was what I wanted to be a part of. I experienced something that had been missing in the painting business: real, meaningful, one-on-one personal impact.

After a two-year detour into financial advising (I know, I know—I told you it was a long path), I finally enrolled in dental school at the age of twenty-nine and started down the path to building my own practice. I graduated at thirty-three, completed a residency at the VA hospital, worked in a Medicaid practice, and moved through a few corporate practices. Deep down, I always knew I wanted to start my own practice to get back to that meaningful one-on-one connection that had brought me into dentistry in the first place. So eventually, that's what I did.

Now, if your dental school was anything like mine, you probably spent more time memorizing the citric acid cycle or studying the chemical components of biomaterials than learning how to run a practice. I, for one, am constantly finding opportunities to diagnose, treat, and follow-up on the use of acetyl-CoA as it combines with 4-carbon compound oxaloacetate to form 6C citrate!

And therein lies the problem. While we were being forced into the deepest wells of biochemistry, we weren't learning the fundamentals of business. Even with a business degree and having run a large multi-division contracting company, I still needed to learn the specifics of running a dental practice. And even then, I had to learn how to run one that was both profitable and fulfilling. That last point is the kicker, and it's something many dentists unfortunately never achieve. There were plenty of times I thought I would never achieve it either.

All this to say, if you feel like your practice is running you, that's okay. You're not alone—in fact, you're probably in the majority. One of my coaching clients, Richard, spent several years as a traveling dentist where he would travel around the country doing procedures that were out of the scope of certain practices. For a long time, he didn't want his own practice because he saw the same things over and over again in all the different practices he visited. More often than not, the practice owned the dentist, and he figured if he were to open his own, then the same thing would happen to him.

When he finally switched gears and bought an established practice, that *is* essentially what happened to him. He spent about two years in panic mode, working long hours and fighting to keep it afloat. Once I met him and he told me about what he was going through, I knew I had to help in some way. Now, after coaching him for the past nine months, he's gotten things under control. He's still got some work to do, but he's now running his practice instead of it running him. (Nearly all the methods I've helped him implement are in this book—you'll hear his name come up a few times.)

The systems in our industry have been shaped in many ways to put the dentist last, and in some instances, it feels like they were even built to take advantage of the dentist. The good news is that this skill gap can be bridged. Right now, you might feel like a dentist who owns a practice or even a dentist who's owned by their practice. *It doesn't have to be that way.* You have the skill set to run a fulfilling seven-figure practice. I know this because I've gone down the same path that you have, and it isn't an easy one.

You have an immense capacity to learn. You have an immense capacity to care. You have an immense capacity to work hard. When you put those things together with the right information and the right guidance, you can enact dramatic change in your life and practice.

The first task? Shift your paradigm from being "a dentist who owns a practice" to a *healthcare entrepreneur*. A healthcare entrepreneur is someone who realizes that there's so much more to owning a dental practice than just production. They take control of the business, understand how it's run, and have the knowledge and confidence to steer the practice in the direction of their choosing. A healthcare entrepreneur understands that there are three fundamental components to running a successful dental practice: *leadership, management, and marketing.*

In this book, I will teach you how to master those three domains by implementing tried-and-true business principles—some of which are specific to the dental industry and some of which will apply to nearly any business. I'll show you, in detail, how to implement these tactics into your practice and provide examples to illustrate their effectiveness. These are lessons I've learned through my own failures, from my mentors, or through my own extensive research. I've tested them in the real world through my own practice and through the practices of my coaching clients.

The upshot? If you're looking to transform your current dental practice or build a new one that's profitable, fulfilling, enjoyable, and protects your time, you're in the right place. And yes, seven figures is achievable.

How to Read This Book

Method #1: The Bookshelf. Buy the book, place it on the bookshelf, and say you'll read it later. If this is you, then you probably didn't get this far anyway. At least the cover is pretty awesome.

Method #2: Edu-tainment. I understand that some people like reading stuff about their industry with no real intentions of implementing the advice. If that's you, I hope my stories will be entertaining enough to keep you going. And maybe you'll walk away with some information that will improve your life or practice. This is an unintentional approach, but an approach nonetheless. Read it and see what happens!

Method #3: The Pearls Approach. Read the book and look for a few "pearls" that you can apply to your life and practice. Find a couple aha moments that give you motivation to make some changes. If this is you, feel free to jump around from topic to topic or skip right to the stuff that interests you most. While I'm not opposed to this strategy, I must warn you: You might be confused at certain points.

Method #4: Intentional Transformation. This book is meant to be read from introduction to conclusion, and the advice is meant to be implemented. The first chapters create the foundation for what comes next, and so on. Throughout the book, you'll also find areas where I recommend writing things down or completing an exercise. If you're intentional about soaking up the knowledge and doing the work in each chapter, you'll not only be able to create the blueprint for your seven-figure practice—you'll actually achieve it. If this is you, then you're my people.

The reality is that if you want to have this type of practice and lifestyle, it's going to take a lot of hard intentional work. As such, I wrote this book for people who want to intentionally change their lives and work hard to achieve their goals. I often say that life is going to be hard either way; you just get to choose what type of hard. So which one will you choose? The hard life that burns you out and brings you down with no end in sight, or the hard life that results in more fulfillment, purpose, and a thriving business? I think you know the answer.

Part One

LEADERSHIP

DRAFTING YOUR BLUEPRINT

I love my town of Wilmington, North Carolina for so many reasons. One of them is that we're blessed with an amazing coastline and some world-class fishing. It's unique in that there's a huge variety of species here, with fish you'd expect to find in southern Florida (like redfish and cobia) as well as up north in New England (like striped bass). Now, I wouldn't say I'm an expert fisherman, but I do enjoy getting out with my friends a few times per month. It's something we all look forward to.

If you've ever gone deep-sea fishing, you'll know there's a lot of preparation involved. My friends and I will spend the whole week talking about what we're going to fish for, the weather and wave forecast, and who is bringing what. On Friday night, we'll get our equipment ready. The next morning, we'll show up at the dock around 5:00 a.m. to load up the boat. And when I say "load up the boat," I mean make sure we've got enough donuts, coffee, ice, and assorted beverages to get through the day. We've got the whole routine pretty dialed in—except for what happens next.

After we leave the dock and make it to open water, someone inevitably pipes up and asks, "So, where are we going?"

"Huh. I don't know! Do you?"

"Well, no... I thought you knew!"

"*I* don't know!"

We have the gear. We have the right tackle and bait. We have the donuts, we're drinking the coffee, and the beer is on ice. We have an extremely sophisticated GPS that can navigate us to any corner of the ocean. But for some reason, none of us have thought to set a waypoint. *We don't know where we're going.* We don't even know where we're *supposed* to go!

Let me tell you, you can have all the best gear in the world, but if you don't know where to go or how to get there, you're not going to catch many fish.

Course-Correcting

In life, there's no GPS, but there is a destination. Too often, people go through life without a clear direction or destination in mind. They go through the motions each day with no plan, just hoping that things will work out in the end. Surprisingly, this is extremely common for dentists.

It has nothing to do with intelligence—there's no denying that you have to be pretty darn intelligent to get through dental school. It just has to do with the fact that for most of our lives, we've been told exactly what to do, how to do it, where to be, and what's coming next. We've spent years jumping through hoops and checking off a list of predetermined tasks in dental school, or in residency, or working in someone else's practice.

So, naturally, when it comes time to open our own practice—the "final" step in our journey, the one we've been waiting so long for—we do what we think we're *supposed* to do. We go through the motions yet again, and more often than not, we end up with a practice that runs us. If you're feeling like your dental practice runs you, then I'm here to tell you that course-correcting is entirely possible.

More than that, it's the point of this book. As the owner of a dental practice, you have an opportunity to build the life of your dreams—and it's not too late.

Speaking of which, I'm happy to tell you that my friends and I have also course-corrected. We now make it a point to clarify the exact GPS coordinates we'll be navigating to *the night before* we head out on the water. This has solved most of our problems—except for the time I hit south instead of north while inputting our coordinates and the GPS started navigating us 3,000 miles into the southern hemisphere. That mistake took a shockingly long time to realize. (It was cloudy! Give me a break.)

This book is about building a seven-figure dental practice that supports you in having the life of your dreams. But in order to do this, you first need to know what the life of your dreams looks like! That's why the first step in our journey has nothing to do with business tactics or even business itself. It's about you. *What do you ultimately want?* And are you headed in the right direction, or do you need to adjust? This kind of questioning might get uncomfortable. Maybe you have some thoughts around this, but you've been suppressing them for a long time—thoughts like, "Yeah, I always *wanted* to travel the world, but that's just unrealistic. I have a life here." It's not unrealistic. Nothing is off-limits.

While the title of this book is *The Seven-Figure Practice Blueprint for Dentists*, there should really be a asterisk there. Because we're not just creating the blueprint for your ideal practice; we're creating the blueprint for your ideal life. The two are inherently intertwined, no matter how much you might want to separate them. And that's okay, because if you do the work in this book, you'll reach a point where you love your practice. Where it's a *great* part of your life. Where you enjoy going to work every day. Sounds nice, doesn't it?

But like any blueprint, you have to start by getting your vision down on the page. We're going to do that using a framework I call "define, refine, implement"—or DRI for short. Spoiler alert: You're going to hear this phrase a *lot* during our time together.

Define, Refine, Implement

DRI is a framework or mental map that I've created for thinking through complex problems or situations. At a high level, the idea is to *define* what you want to achieve, *refine* the system you'll use to achieve it, and then *implement* the system after it's been created. It can be used for big-picture vision-type work where you're setting personal and professional goals far into the future, all the way down to granular decisions on whether or not to implement a new procedure.

Here's how it works:

DEFINE: Create a clear picture of the outcome you desire.

REFINE: Analyze your current state compared to your defined outcome to determine what needs to be eliminated, added, or changed to achieve your goal. This process typically involves creating a system that will increase the likelihood of achieving what you've defined that you want. It's also the most time-intensive part.

IMPLEMENT: Put into action what you've determined as the best practice for your life and practice. This might sound obvious, but without action there will be no progress toward your desired outcome—you'll either go nowhere or find yourself somewhere you didn't want to go in the first place.

This framework can be applied to practically anything. Really, it's just a simple way to carefully think through any big change or initiative. If you wanted to build your dream home, for example, you'd probably follow the DRI framework without even realizing it:

DEFINE: Create a clear vision for your dream house.

REFINE: Turn that vision into an architectural blueprint that will bring your dream house to life.

IMPLEMENT: Build the house by following your blueprint.

The last element to the DRI framework is to "repeat as necessary." If you're not getting the outcome you desire, you can repeat the DRI framework by *redefining* the outcome you want, *further refining* the system, and then *implementing the new changes* that have come out of that process. When we get into business systems, you'll see how this framework can be used to revisit many of the processes in your practice.

You know how there's that one thing you have to do that's annoying, isn't a good use of your time, or just isn't "working" for whatever reason? Well, you can always go back and use the DRI framework to re-create the system and achieve your desired outcome. I do this in my own life and with my clients on a routine basis: revisiting systems to make sure the defined goals are still appropriate, the systems in place are adequate, and the systems are being correctly implemented. This allows for course correction and confirms we're moving closer to that ideal practice.

My goal isn't for you to write out the entire framework every time you want to implement something in your business (although that could be helpful in some cases), but to adopt the *mindset* of DRI so you can think through what you want and how to best achieve it before you get to implementation. That might sound obvious, but I can't tell you how often we skip these crucial steps. When you're busy, or when you're excited about some new opportunity, or when you just need to get things *done*, it's all too easy to skip those two crucial steps of defining and refining. When it becomes a mindset, you'll instinctively think through the steps as you go, leading to more effective implementation that consistently gets you closer to your desired outcomes.

At a high level, even the structure of this book follows the DRI framework. We're going to start by defining what you want to achieve with your life and dental practice. Then, I'll walk you through all the various tactics and strategies required to build a seven-figure dental practice so you can determine what needs to be eliminated, added, or changed in your own life to achieve your goal. By the end, with your blueprint in hand, you'll be ready to successfully implement those changes in your life and with your team.

So, with that said, we're going to dive right into the first step of DRI by *defining* what you are looking to achieve and where you want to go. There are three key components to this process that will give you direction and guidance throughout your journey to a seven-figure practice: your *vision*, *mission*, and *core values*.

Vision

Your vision just might be the most important concept we'll discuss in this book. Everything that comes after this will ultimately relate back to your vision, which I define as *the aspirational destination for your life*.

Remember in the introduction when I talked about getting home at 8:45 p.m. and missing my kids' bedtime and drinking too much? I was in that situation because I never intentionally set a vision for my life. If you never define your vision, you're likely to operate in ways that are counterproductive toward your goals—even inadvertently. You might not notice those counterproductive actions in the short-term, but you'll look back and realize their consequences over the long-term. Only by then, it will be too late to do anything about it. You have to be intentional. The time to start is now.

One way to think of your vision is the "end goal" of your life. If you were to think ahead and imagine your ideal life in the future, the picture you paint for yourself is your vision. It's aspirational in that it should be something you're striving toward—it might even seem impossible at the moment. It's also inward-facing in that it's kind of all about you. This is what *you* want to achieve for yourself. It can—and likely will—include other people, but it's ultimately your decision to make. It's the one time to truly look at yourself in the mirror and say, "What do *I* want?"

> **NOTE:** This book is called *The Seven-Figure Practice Blueprint for Dentists*. While I'm a dentist and most of the examples are dentist-specific, any healthcare entrepreneur can benefit from this book.

Having a vision creates forward clarity in your life. I say it's the most important concept in the book because, at the end of the day, if you don't know where you want to go, I can't help you. If you don't have a clear vision in place, you're just going to end up . . . somewhere. It's like building a house with no blueprint; just plodding along and hoping you end up with a house that isn't going to fall down on top of you. I don't have to tell you how that's going to go.

Your vision will dictate nearly everything you do from this point onward. Not only will it affect the decisions you make in your personal life and in your practice, but it will also ensure that you're taking the right actions every day to move toward the life you desire.

And as with many of the exercises we'll cover in this book, I'm going to ask that you write your vision down. It should be a concise statement (one or two sentences) on what you want to achieve in your life. Specificity is key here. I suspect most people have some idea of their ideal life or where they'd like to end up, but few actually take the time to specify what that vision looks like and put it in writing. A vague idea isn't going to get you where you want to go because it's simply not enough to dictate your decisions and behavior on a daily basis. Without specificity, you're likely to slip. We're faced with so many decisions and so many paths in life that it's easy to slip into what's easiest, what makes sense in the moment, or what your impulses are telling you to do. A clear, concise vision is the number-one key to navigating these situations and ensuring that you're moving in the right direction over the long-term.

MY VISION:
People will experience the love of Christ when they interact with me.

This personal vision came out of hours and hours of reading, journaling, and reflecting on where my priorities lie and what matters most in my life. I intentionally committed time to this process because I saw the value of having a concise vision statement that captures the long-term goal of my life.

My vision is ultimately what I want to achieve in my life and the legacy I want to leave behind. My vision guides me on a daily basis. It's what I'm striving to become. It's also extremely clear to me; when I read those words, I know exactly what they mean. And yes, it does involve religion. I'm a Christian and the love of Christ is something that's important to me. Your vision is ultimately about what's important to you—if you're not religious, then it probably isn't going to include religion. If you are and it's important to you, maybe it will. It's entirely up to you. This is *your* vision and no one else's.

Below are a few examples of personal vision statements from prominent figures of the past.

- **Nelson Mandela:** To create a society where all people live together in harmony and with equal opportunities.
- **Mahatma Gandhi:** To see a world where truth and non-violence reign supreme.
- **Martin Luther King Jr.:** To see a world where people are judged by the content of their character, not the color of their skin.
- **Eleanor Roosevelt:** To ensure that every person has the opportunity to achieve their fullest potential and to participate in and contribute to all aspects of life.
- **Mother Teresa:** "To serve the poorest of the poor and to see Christ in every person I meet."

So, how exactly can you create your vision statement? Well, for some people it may come naturally—perhaps you already have something in mind. For others, it can be more difficult. Either way, I often use the following exercise with my coaching clients to help them think through their vision.

Vision Exercise

It might sound a bit morbid, but one way to start thinking about your vision is to write your own eulogy. A eulogy describes how someone is remembered, what they achieved in their life, and how they made people feel. It's a great way to think about what you ultimately want out of your life, and it can help you get clear on what's most important in life *now*, rather than at the end of it.

You probably don't want the person giving your eulogy to say, "They were known for making tons of money and running a highly efficient dental practice," right? Those could be goals you want to achieve in your life, but they are not your *vision*. Your vision is bigger than that.

To start this exercise, imagine yourself at the end of a long, fulfilling life. What would you want people to say about you? What accomplishments would you be most proud of? What impact would you want to leave on the world? What legacy would you leave?

Imagine sitting in the back of the room at your own funeral, listening to someone you care deeply about giving your eulogy. Write down what you'd want them to say. Try to be as specific and detailed as possible. This is easier than you think—it will probably start flowing out of you naturally. And keep in mind that this is personal. Sure, there might be some aspects related to your dentistry practice ("They were a great dentist and their patients loved them"), but this is about your personal relationships, your life accomplishments, your character, maybe your involvement in your local community—it's all up to you.

As you're thinking about this, I would also urge you to not get bogged down in what seems "realistic." This is about your ideal vision for your life—so make it ideal. Your vision is something you will strive to achieve over the course of your entire life, and what feels unrealistic now might not feel so unrealistic after 30 or 40 years of incremental improvements. Don't limit yourself! If you want to be remembered for starting a charitable foundation or impacting the lives of millions of people, write it down.

Your eulogy may start as one or a few paragraphs. It can be as long as you'd like, but the next step is to review that information and clarify what's truly important to you. If you could only preserve one or a few things from all that text, what would it be? What's the

TIP: You can find downloadable templates for this and many of the exercises in this book at **www.drbenfriberg.com/bookresources**.

one big, overarching theme? This is a challenging step because your natural inclination is that *everything* you wrote down is important. Think carefully, cut the stuff that isn't absolutely vital, and turn that into one clear, concise statement. That's now your vision, which you'll write down and commit to memory.

If we were to think about this within the DRI framework, the first step would be to *define* the need for a personal vision in your life. Without defining that need, you'll never see the importance of this exercise or benefit from your vision statement. The *refine* step would then be to go through the eulogy exercise to clarify what you ultimately want to achieve in your life. You can then *implement* your vision by writing it down and living it out. (You'll accomplish this last step in large part by creating a successful practice that gives you the freedom to live your vision!)

If you'd like, you can write your vision in the space below.

My vision: _____.

Mission

While your vision is aspirational and inward-facing, your mission is practical and outward-facing. This becomes especially valuable when combined with a set of core values, which we'll cover next. Another way to think about this is that your vision is "what" you're building, and your mission and core values are "how" you're going to build it. I like to define mission as *what you're actively doing now to achieve your vision*. It's about the change you want to make in the world around you. It informs the way you behave and the impact you have on those you interact with. If you were to follow it daily, it should lead you to achieving your vision.

As an example, here are personal mission statements from some prominent leaders:

Oprah Winfrey: "To be a teacher. And to be known for inspiring my students to be more than they thought they could be."
Maya Angelou: "My mission in life is not merely to survive, but to thrive; and to do so with some passion, some compassion, some humor, and some style."
Richard Branson: "To have fun in my journey through life and learn from my mistakes."

My mission: To inspire those around me to become the best versions of themselves through empathy, encouragement, and insight. I will improve myself daily, make myself available to others, and maintain a passion for the success of those I engage with.

As you think about your own mission, the goal should be to settle on something that's achievable on a daily basis. If it's not achievable on a daily basis, it might sound nice, but it won't generate much in the way of results. Those big, aspirational missions you hear like "Helping one million people live a healthier life" or "To accelerate progress and drive innovation in [insert industry here]"? Yeah, those sound great—but they're not exactly practical. You can't help a million people every day, and watching that ticker go up isn't going to be very motivating. What will be motivating, however, is setting out each day knowing you can (and likely will) accomplish your mission.

Mission Exercise

A personal mission statement is a concise declaration that guides your decisions and actions. It's like a roadmap for daily life, helping you stay true to yourself and focused on what truly matters. Here's a guide to how you can create your mission statement using the DRI framework (and remember, you can download a template for this at www.drbenfriberg.com/bookresources).

Define

- **Core Beliefs:** Identify the principles that guide your life. These could be integrity, compassion, innovation, etc. List them out.
- **Passions:** Consider the activities and topics that ignite your enthusiasm. What do you enjoy doing? What causes do you care deeply about? These aren't hobbies, they're more altruistic—like service, giving, making an impact. Note these down.
- **Goals:** Think about what you want to achieve. This could include both personal and professional aspirations. Be specific and clear about your objectives. This isn't about money; it's about the type of legacy you want to leave and the impact you want to make.

Refine

- **Draft Your Statement:** Combine your core values, passions, and goals into a concise statement. Aim for one to two sentences that capture the essence of who you are and what you aim to accomplish.
- **Review and Edit:** Revisit your draft and refine it. Ensure that it's clear, concise, and reflective of your true self. It should resonate with you deeply.

Implement

- **Live by Your Statement:** Use your mission statement as a guide in your daily life. Make decisions and take actions that align with your mission.
- **Revisit and Revise:** As you grow and evolve, your mission statement might need adjustment. Periodically review it to ensure it remains relevant and reflective of your current self.

Creating a personal mission statement is an empowering process that can bring clarity to your daily life. Take your time with it, and let it be a true reflection of who you are and who you aspire to be. When you're ready, you can write it down in the space below.

My mission: _____
_____
_____.

Core Values

Your mission becomes especially powerful when combined with a set of *core values*. Having already established your vision and mission, you have a great start for creating your core values. You'll now drill down deeper into the elements of your character that you want to be evident in your daily decisions and actions. Core values define the type of person you want to be and what you stand for. I define core values as *the fundamental standards that define your character and guide your behavior.* When followed, they should ensure you're a living example of your mission. In this way, you can use them as a frame of reference to help you make decisions that ensure you stay true to who you want to be.

My core values:

1. Integrity: I can be relied upon to withstand the demands and stressors I encounter without sacrificing my ethics and values.
2. Altruism: I will practice selfless concern for the well-being of others.
3. Generosity: I will use the blessings in my life to give time, energy, and money.
4. Growth: I will pursue bettering myself through physical, mental, spiritual, and financial self-improvement and inspire those around me to do the same.
5. Focus: I will pursue the ruthless elimination of distraction to use my time with intention in pursuit of my goals and values.

Not long ago, I was faced with a situation that tested these values—specifically, my core value of integrity. My son was graduating from elementary school and I'd emailed my office manager to schedule time off on a Tuesday morning so I could attend. Unfortunately, my wires were crossed when I sent the email, and I gave her the wrong day. So when the morning of the graduation came, I had a full schedule of patients and hygiene was booked. I had to make a decision. It was tough in the moment. I had to weigh the demands of the practice versus the honor of being present for my son. I went back and forth on what to do and talked to my family about my mistake. They understood and said it wasn't a big deal to miss it. On my way to work, driving past my son's school, I knew I'd chosen poorly. I'd put my practice before my family. I called the office 30 minutes before my first patient would arrive and canceled my morning. My team had to reschedule 14 patients.

My first core value is *integrity*: I can be relied upon to withstand the demands and stresses I encounter without sacrificing my ethics and values. Part of my ethics and values is being there for my family no matter what, so this made my decision obvious. I wrestled with this decision, but in the end it would've been against my core values—against who I am as a person and what I stand for—to miss my son's graduation. Looking back, I'm proud of the decision I made, and I know I would've regretted going into work that morning.

Sometimes in life, the answer is obvious because you're dealing with a good solution versus a bad one. Core values are most beneficial when there are two good decisions to consider—which happens often. Do I honor my commitment to my son and my family, or do I honor my commitment to my practice and my patients? This is how core values help us stick to our blueprint and course correct if we get off track.

Core Values Exercise

Personal core values are the fundamental beliefs that guide your behavior and decisions. They act as a moral compass, helping you navigate life's challenges and opportunities. Here's a guide to defining, refining, and implementing your personal core values.

Define

- **Identify Core Values:** Reflect on what principles are most important to you. Consider values such as integrity, empathy, creativity, resilience, etc. List them out.
- **Prioritize Values:** Rank your list based on their importance in your life. This will help you focus on the values that truly define you.
- **Seek Input:** Ask trusted friends or family members for their perspective on what they see as your core values. This can provide additional insights.

Refine

- **Draft a Values Statement:** Write a brief statement for each value, explaining why it's important to you and how it influences your life.
- **Reflect and Edit:** Revisit your statements and refine them to ensure they accurately reflect your beliefs and aspirations. Make sure they are clear and concise.

Implement

- **Live by Your Values:** Use your core values as a guide in your daily life. Make decisions and take actions that align with your values.
- **Revisit and Revise:** Periodically review your core values to ensure they remain relevant as you grow and evolve. Adjust them if necessary to reflect your current self.

Defining personal core values is a powerful exercise that can bring clarity and direction to your life. These core values serve as a foundation for your decisions, helping you stay true to yourself and live a fulfilling life. Take your time with this process and let your values genuinely reflect who you are. It can be very beneficial to share these core values with your close family, friends, and even your team.

These three exercises—vision, mission, and core values—are just a small upfront effort that will have a massive payoff in the long run. You won't see a difference in your life overnight. You may not even see a difference in your life a month from now—but that's okay, because this is all about incremental progress. It's like an investment account. If you put a small amount of money in right now, you might not see any major growth in the months or years ahead. thirty years from now, you'll be glad you made that first deposit.

Creating Your Blueprint

If you're serious about changing your life, then be intentional about crafting your own mission, vision, and core values. I'm not saying you have to drop everything and get it perfect right now, but I'd like you to at least put pen to paper and start documenting some of your ideas. That's my prescription, but the way you go about it is up to you. I'm not going to tell you there's one specific way you should craft your vision, because there are many different methods and techniques you could use. In fact, I'd urge you to do a bit of your own research to find a method that works for you. And if you'd rather just come up with something entirely on your own, that's fine too. These are for *you*. They should be uniquely you.

That being said, if you're looking for more guidance, I have a few suggestions. The methods that follow are just some examples of how you can start formulating your vision, mission, and core values. I've used them myself and with my clients, and I can vouch for their effectiveness.

Your Decision-Making Framework

Like nearly everything we'll discuss in this book, your vision, mission, and core values are only useful *if you use them*. These are not some phrases you'll write down and throw in a drawer, never to be seen again. These are meant to become the guiding principles for your life.

The best way to start implementing these in your own life is to use them as a decision-making framework. Any time you're faced with a decision, big or small, you can ask yourself, "Is this in line with my vision, mission, and core values?" The answer should be fairly obvious, and if it is—go ahead. Permission granted. If not, that's a sign you should think more carefully about how you want to proceed.

I'll give you an example. When I started Thrive Family Dental, it was with the goal of opening multiple locations. As you'll read later in the book, I created robust systems, a stand-apart brand, and strong leadership that could withstand expansion. There have been multiple opportunities, interested investors, and a strong drive on my part to pursue this option. In the end, I've decided to place that goal on hold. Why? My vision, mission, and core values.

Opening multiple practices would dramatically increase my stress inside and outside of work. I don't want to be a husband and father who's working constantly. I don't want to be home but never "present" because I'm too stressed or tired to engage with my family or too busy sending emails and texts to get things done. It isn't in my vision, mission, or core values to miss out on spontaneous dance routines by my daughter or a couple rounds of my son's favorite video game. There may be a time later in my life when I make the decision to pull the trigger and expand. If it can be done in a way that's aligned with my vision, mission, and core values, I'll do it.

As a dentist, you'll be surrounded by opportunities to make big purchases that make you feel great; purchases that expand your business, influence, or impact. These decisions, even the ones that seem perfect, each come with their own set of consequences. Your vision, mission, and core values should serve as the guiding principles to make sure you're making the right decisions for what you want to achieve in your life.

That said, you don't need to reserve these guiding principles solely for major decisions. Really, these should be the filter you put *all* decisions through, from how you interact with people to how you spend your time. Intentionally using these principles on a daily basis is the best way to stick to this blueprint we're creating. And the best part is it's going to be easy, because they are about who *you* are as a person and what *you* want. If you trust your intuition and are honest with yourself as you refine these principles, you'll naturally want to follow them.

Define, Refine, Implement

Define: Identify and put into words your bigger picture for your life—what you want and how you want to live.

Refine: Create your personal vision, mission, and core values.

Implement: Share your vision, mission, and core values with those close to you (your family, friends, team—whoever you feel most comfortable with) and use them as guiding principles in your daily life.

MAKING YOUR LIFE CONCRETE

I love concrete. Yes, I realize how strange that sounds, but concrete is an amazing substance because it can be used to create just about anything. As a result, our world is practically made up of concrete—in fact, it's one of the most-consumed materials in the world, second only to water.[i] Around the world, twice as much concrete is used in construction as all other building materials *combined*.

The fascinating thing about concrete is that it's made up of simple elements that are nearly worthless as building materials on their own—sand, cement, gravel, and water—but with the right know-how and process, you can turn those elements into amazing structures that will stand the test of time. A skyscraper. A home. A factory. A dental practice! Concrete is *so* much bigger than the sum of its parts, and so are you.

In this chapter, we're going to be exploring the idea of a *concrete life*. Just like an architect can make their wildest visions come true through the magic of concrete, you can create anything you want out of your life. But how does this actually happen in your case? Well, there will be a lot of steps to get there—many of which we'll be covering in detail later—but the first thing is setting your foundation. A dental practice needs a solid foundation, and I'm not talking about your physical office. I'm talking about you. As the owner of your practice, you are the foundation—and everything starts with you. You're the concrete, which means you can make anything happen.

However, let's consider the other side of this coin. It's often said that with great power comes great responsibility. While you have the power to create the life you want through your dental practice, you also have an important responsibility to get this right. It's all on you. A concrete foundation is great if it's done right, but if the materials aren't mixed in the right quantities or if it sits too long before being used, it can do more harm than good.

Nothing illustrates this dichotomy better than the story of the Big Dig—the most expensive highway project in United States history. This is when, in 1991, the city of Boston decided to reroute their highway underground, running it directly beneath the city's downtown. The highway was previously routed through the city on an elevated platform called the Central Artery. This platform was not only unsightly, but it also caused a whole host of problems—interestingly enough, it may even be the cause of the stereotypes surrounding Boston's "aggressive" drivers, as there was no breakdown lane and the on-off ramps were so short that drivers had to fight tooth and nail to get on and off.

The Big Dig was an amazing feat of engineering, and as you can imagine, it used a *lot* of concrete—*135,000 truckloads* to be exact.[ii] Besides moving a highway underground, it also involved creating an enormous suspension bridge, rerouting an interchange of multiple highways, building tunnels under the ocean, and even *freezing the ground* at one point because the soil was too unstable to build a tunnel. All made of concrete. Incredible.

Now, with any building project like this, there are tests that need to be done and logged to ensure every truckload of concrete is structurally sound. And having worked in this world myself, the idea of all 135,000 truckloads of concrete being structurally sound is . . .

a little unrealistic. Long after the project had been completed, this was confirmed when two people paid the price. They were driving through a tunnel when a piece of concrete fell from the roof and hit their car, killing one of them and injuring the other.

Later, after multiple investigations, it came out that the company responsible for producing the concrete hadn't done the required tests and had falsified their records to cover it up. In his testimony, one of the quality-control technicians said that he "[couldn't] swear under oath that even one truckload was batched as it should have been." The construction and engineering teams were overwhelmed, so they rushed and cut corners. Unfortunately, the cost was a human life.

This stuff is important. In your line of work, lives are on the line—you're prescribing and administering drugs that could have potentially lethal effects on people. Your patients' oral health is, of course, on the line—as are your team members' livelihoods, your family's well-being, and your standing in the community. The concrete life is about intentionally setting the right foundation—physically, mentally, financially, and spiritually—for your life so you are operating at peak performance. Having the right foundation will set you up to make better decisions, work harder, lead better, and ultimately run a successful practice. It also benefits everyone around you because you'll be operating at your best. Anything less than that is a missed opportunity.

The good news for you is that unlike the Big Dig, you can always go back and adjust your foundation. Whatever mistakes you've made up to this point, whatever bad habits you've acquired, don't worry—it can all be fixed, and we can do it together.

Strength and Integrity

The Big Dig is a perfect example of what can happen when you don't care about doing things right; when you don't put the effort in or have the integrity to do things the right way; when you take shortcuts or neglect responsibilities. Those decisions might seem fine initially—they might even seem like the only feasible option at the time—but they'll catch up with you in the end.

Running a successful practice always comes back to the strength and integrity of the owner-dentist. You need to be ready for the trials and tribulations of running a business *plus* the rigors of being a dentist. You'll be feeling stress from many places—your patients, your team, your finances, your marketing company, your vendors—and you need to have the strength to deal with that. You also need to have the integrity to make the right decisions for yourself, your patients, and your team. If we think back to the Big Dig, the people making that concrete lacked integrity—they were operating in a way that wasn't in the best interest of those who'd be using that tunnel. And the concrete lacked strength because of those decisions.

We've created the blueprint for your ideal life and practice. Now, it's time to *build* that life. That means putting the right pieces together in the right way and taking it seriously. If you really want to do this, you need to have the integrity to do the right thing and the strength to withstand all the trials and tribulations that will happen to you on this journey. Because, trust me, you will be tested. It's time to get serious and build a lifestyle that's in harmony with your vision.

You're a Professional Athlete

Just to put things into perspective here, consider this: As a dentist, you have the income potential of a professional athlete. And I'm not talking about some third-string special teams player fresh out of college; I'm talking about the big bucks.

And the similarities don't stop at income. If you've made it to the point where you're even considering opening your own practice, that means you've also put in the work of a professional athlete. You've put in your 10,000 hours (or much more). *You're kind of a big deal.* People think professional athletes are rare, and that only a very select few make it to that level. Guess what? The same applies to dentists. Becoming a dentist is a long, arduous road—not a lot of people take the first step, and many don't make it to the end. Case in point: As of 2023, there are 202,304 professionally active dentists in the US. That equates to around one dentist for every 2,000 people, meaning we make up 0.06 percent of the population.[iii] There are not a lot of people who have achieved the level of success that you have right now, even if it might not feel like it at the moment.

All of this to say . . . *Act accordingly.*

Professional athletes need to be rigorous about their training, how they eat, avoid injury, and do whatever else is required of them to operate at peak performance. They're not going out drinking every night with their college buddies or hitting McDonald's on the way home because they're feeling lazy. They need to strictly maintain their physical and mental health to perform at the highest level day in and day out. They need to have the mindset of a winner and take extreme ownership over the fact that they're in full control of the outcome of their career.

Professional athletes are forced to take their job seriously because if they don't, someone else is going to take their place. One of my patients is a professional athlete, and out of curiosity I asked about his training regimen. It was more detailed than I could've imagined. He has a velocity-based strength coach, a physical therapist, and a genetics-based nutritionist—and that's not including all the other coaches who work with him inside of the team. He's surrounded himself with experts to get the most out of his career. He understands that his performance is his number-one asset, and he acts accordingly.

Running a dental practice isn't a nine-to-five job that you can mindlessly clock in and out of. It's not something you can coast through. You need to take it seriously, just like a professional athlete takes their sport seriously. (Because, by the way, you are a "professional" in the literal sense of the word.) And I'll even take it one step further to say that what you're doing is *more important and impactful* than what professional athletes are doing. It's not even a question—you're providing care for people. You're alleviating their pain. You're in charge of their health.

That's serious business, so act accordingly. What you do outside of the office, your physical health, how you conduct yourself—it all affects your performance as a dentist and business owner. It affects your strength and integrity.

The Dentist as the Foundation

The first step of any building project is the foundation. The foundation needs to be strong enough to withstand everything that gets built on top of it—it needs to have the right structure, the right materials, and be put together in the right way. *You* are the foundation of your practice. Just like a building foundation, you also need to be strong enough to withstand everything that gets built on top of you. This is important. It's not something you can skip or gloss over.

Because here's the thing: I know dentists. I have a lot of dentist friends, and I mentor dentists in two different mastermind groups. (For context, I run my own personal mastermind group, the Thrive Collective, that works with dentists of all specialties, and I'm also employed by Ideal Practices to run their mastermind, which caters specifically to start-up dentists.) Every dentist I know understands how important physical health is. With our knowledge of the body, we don't need someone to tell us about the importance of exercise or eating right or avoiding smoking.

Yet *many* dentists don't prioritize their own health. They aren't intentional about it. They know what they should be doing, but they let things slip because they're busy, because they need to focus on their practice—whatever it is. We have plenty of excuses just like everyone else—probably even more than the average person. That can't happen. You have to intentionally maintain your health in order to operate your practice at the level required to achieve seven figures. Period. It's nonnegotiable. It has to be a priority, just like you'd prioritize the dental health of your patients.

Now, I'm not going to tell you how to exercise or preach to you about why you should be taking omega-3 fatty acids (which you should be). What I am going to do is drill into your head how this stuff relates to a seven-figure practice. Just like there are four ingredients in concrete, there are four ingredients of your health that you need to intentionally prioritize to develop a strong foundation for your practice. Those four ingredients are as follows:

1. Physical Health
2. Mental Health
3. Financial Health
4. Spiritual Health

Let's take a look at each.

Physical Health

For professional athletes, their body is their livelihood. And really, the same applies to dentists. Sure, we're not running forty-yard dashes, but we are doing a physical job. I like to say we're the "blue-collar doctor." We're doing construction of the mouth. We're hunched over, putting our bodies in strange positions for thirty or more hours per week over the course of twenty, thirty, forty years. This takes a physical toll. In fact, around 30 percent of dentists retire early due to neck and back problems.[iv]

You need to be responsible for your health to make sure you're capable of doing the more physical parts of dentistry—and specifically, doing them without pain for a long time. I'm confident that you understand the fundamentals of how to do this. If you smoke, you know you should quit smoking. If you don't exercise, you know you should be exercising. My recommendation is to find some type of exercise that works for you and that you like doing.

One of my clients is really into CrossFit. He built his own gym, and he makes his own workouts every day and posts them online—he's an absolute beast. Personally, that's not my thing. I don't enjoy that type of exercise, and if that's what I had to do every day, I'd hate exercising. For me, I prefer long cardio. I *love* going on a three- or four-hour-long bike ride (which my client would hate, by the way). I'm actually training for an Ironman as I write this, and I look forward to that training, which means exercise isn't something I'll ever put off. I prioritize it. If you can find that thing, you'll do well.

Remember my client Richard from the introduction? He wasn't working out consistently when I first started working with him, but he had aspirations of building a home gym. Through our work together, I helped him prioritize that, and he now has a space where he likes to go and exercise. He's told me how much of a difference it's made in his performance—not just physically, but mentally, as it helps him recharge. He's also in incredible shape now, for the record.

Another dentist I coached was a little different. He was under an immense amount of stress with his practice. I'd sometimes look at all the things on his plate and wonder how he coped with it. Turns out, alcohol was his coping mechanism. He'd been drinking at least two to three scotches a night for nearly twenty years. He had trouble falling asleep, so he frequently took sleeping medication. He wasn't exercising at all.

When we talked about it, he knew this wasn't sustainable. He knew he had to make a change—like I said, you can't get to our level of education and remain ignorant about these things. We talked it through, and I helped him make some gradual changes. As of this writing, he hasn't had a drink for around three weeks. He lives on the water, and every morning he's gotten up and jumped in the ocean. He spends four minutes doing cold therapy, then he goes on a two-mile walk. Shortly after starting, he told me that he was able to fall asleep without drinking or medication for the first time in fifteen years.

This isn't a physical training book—although that does give me some ideas for my next one—so I'm not going to get into the exact details on what types of exercise you should be doing. If you're unclear on this or not feeling up to the task, my recommendation would be to find a physical therapist or athletic trainer who can help increase your strength and mobility. That's what I have, and it's worked out well for me.

Also, if you're experiencing back pain from dentistry, a foam roller does wonders. I have one at home and one at my practice, and I use them constantly.

Mental Health

Running a dental practice can take a real toll on you. You've likely heard that dentists have the highest suicide rate of any profession—more than lawyers, medical doctors, architects, or any other "professional" in the literal sense of the word. In my research for this book, I actually discovered that's not entirely true—but the reality is that the suicide rate for dentists is significant.

I'll say right now that if you're in a place where you're contemplating ending your life, please put this book down right now and seek help. I've worked through this in my own life, and I don't want anybody to ever have to go through that alone. If you're struggling in this way, this book isn't going to fix it—all that matters is that you drop what you're doing and seek professional help. I'd be more than happy to talk to you about what you're going through—just reach out to me via my website at www.drbenfriberg.com. (Seriously.)

That said, if you find yourself feeling anxious, if you're yelling at your team, or if you throw your instruments when you get angry—that behavior isn't okay, and "stress" isn't an adequate excuse. There are likely some underlying issues you need to work on. And if you don't, these things will continue to affect you (and your team and your patients) for the rest of your career. They'll prevent you from running a fulfilling seven-figure practice.

There's an undeniable connection between physical health and the way we feel mentally. Maintaining your physical health will give you greater clarity of thought, creativity, mental health, and a better ability to focus. That all translates to better well-being and better care for your patients. But exercising, as much as I love it, won't solve all your problems.

If you're having any sort of mental health issues that are having a negative impact on your life, it's important to address those head-on in a way that's in line with what you want for your life (your vision, mission, core values). In the introduction, I talked about the period in my life when I was working long hours and was miserable in my dental practice. During that time, I wasn't exercising and I was drinking too much. I had anxiety and anger issues with my family—my kids specifically. I was interacting with them in a way that I wasn't proud of. I wasn't being present with them, I was impatient, and I'd come up with excuses to avoid playing with them. Looking back, I can now see that I wasn't operating in line with my vision, mission, and core values. Not even close.

Eventually, I had a wake-up call and realized I needed to change. So I went to counseling. It was a hard decision. I had to humble myself and come to the realization that I wasn't equipped to face what I was going through on my own. I went and got help.

There are plenty of barriers that hold people back from seeking help in this area—time, money, stigmas around mental health. As healthcare professionals, the biggest barriers for us are typically pride and ego. Due to the nature of our work, we often feel we should be able to handle everything ourselves. But at a certain point, you have to recognize when you're out of your element. We're trained to improve people's oral health, not our own mental health.

When I finally made that decision to get help, I realized that I'd never have gotten out of that situation on my own. Looking back, I can now see how investing time and money in my mental health was no different from investing in continuing education or new equipment for my practice. In fact, it's proven to be one of the most valuable investments I've made—both for myself and my practice.

If you've already created your vision, mission, and core values, then you're a step ahead here. You should be able to look back at your behavior and the feelings you're having and assess whether these are aligned with those guiding principles (unless your vision is to be a jerk, which I'd hope it's not). I'm not a mental health expert, so I won't tell you explicitly what to do. But I will tell you that there are people who can help with these sorts of things—you just need to be intentional and make that initial decision to reach out.

You're Not Alone in This

One of the leading causes of mental health challenges among dentists is what I call the "chasm of isolation." As both a doctor and a business owner, there's no one in your world who truly understands what you're going through other than your fellow practice owners. And this isn't an ego thing—it's an isolation thing. There's a serious knowledge gap, liability gap, financial risk gap, and licensing gap between you and everyone else around you, including your team.

Unlike most business owners who can delegate many aspects of their role, as a dentist, that's not always possible. You're typically the only person in your practice with the education, training, and licensing to do what you do. You can't delegate a root canal to your hygienist because they simply don't have the knowledge, training, and license to do that procedure. That pressure of feeling like you have to do everything on your own can be tough to deal with—even if it's not literally everything.

You also bear unique burdens: the financial risk (most dentists have over a million dollars in debt between dental school, starting their practice, mortgage, etc.), the ever-present liability concerns, and the need to maintain some professional distance from your employees. At the end of the day, you're their boss—you may need to make difficult decisions about their employment one day, so there has to be some level of separation between you and your employees. Everything in your practice starts and ends with you, and that's very isolating.

The best way to address these challenges is by connecting with other owner dentists. End of story. These are the only people who can truly relate to what we're going through. I highly recommend having a community of fellow owner dentists who you can talk about these things with. However, finding the *right* community is key. There are plenty of dentistry groups out there, but unfortunately many of them come with a lot of ego and one-upmanship. If you're in a group of people who only want to show off their skills or prove that they're better than everyone else, that's not helping anyone. I'd avoid those groups and intentionally seek out groups where you can be vulnerable, open, and honest. If you can't find one, consider starting your own—that's what I did!

I created the Thrive Collective, which is a monthly mastermind group for like-minded dentists who want to pursue excellence in their personal lives, their profession, and their community. This is a safe and vulnerable group where everyone brings wisdom and expertise and is dedicated to lifting each other up. I'm super proud of it.

And just to be clear, it doesn't have to be some formal group with a logo and a big yearly conference—even just regularly getting together with some dentist colleagues can provide that crucial outlet. Create a space where you can openly discuss the real challenges: "I'm stressed. Last Monday when I got to work, my schedule was empty. We were 40 percent below cost, and I knew I would lose money if something didn't change." Or where you can ask, "Hey, what trends are you seeing in your practice? How's your new patient flow?"

It's important from a mental health perspective to be able to sit down and talk openly about these things. For a long time, I felt like the things I was going through in my practice weren't "normal," but when I started talking with other dentists, I realized we were all going through the same things. These feelings are almost inevitable because of how the system is designed, and you're only going to have these types of conversations when you have real, authentic relationships with other dentists that go beyond just networking.

Communities are also a great way to get specific advice you won't find anywhere else. Having some fellow dentists to bounce ideas off is incredibly valuable. And you can add value to these groups too—remember that you also have a wealth of knowledge to share, and your involvement will help others just like they'll help you.

Financial Health

Financial health is all-encompassing in that there's no way to untether this from your business—if you're making bad financial decisions in your business, your personal finances will be negatively impacted. But you also need to be clear on your personal financial goals in order to build a business that will fulfill them.

My recommendation here is to work with a financial advisor who's sophisticated enough for the complexity of an owner dentist—not just a dentist and not just a business owner, but a dentist who owns their own practice. They should have experience in this domain. Asking a dentist friend for a recommendation is an easy first step, or you can consult the resource page at drbenfriberg.com/bookresources for a list of my personal recommendations.

This is another one of those areas where I'm confident that you know what to do. Spend less than you earn, save at a rate that will get you to your retirement goals, set aside money for emergencies—this isn't anything new, and if you've made it through dental school, you surely understand these basic principles. But just because you understand them doesn't mean you intentionally practice them in your life. In fact, on average, dentists retire later than the general population even though they have significantly higher income. This is often attributed to "entitlement spending," where dentists feel they need to attain a certain lifestyle and end up spending money on things they don't need or want. It can also be a result of stress, where we think we "deserve" that fancy new object as a reward for all we endure.

Either way, if you continually find yourself buying things you don't need at the detriment of your financial health, then maybe there's an underlying mental health issue causing this behavior. The four aspects of health are interconnected—how you show up in one affects the other, and just like concrete, you need all four components working together to get the best outcome. Poor financial health on a personal level can also have a direct correlation to your practice. If you're struggling financially, and you're feeling this mounting pressure to make more money, you're going to put profit over patients. It's a bit counterintuitive, but this typically ends up hurting your profit in the long run—if you try to get every nickel and dime out of your patients, they're going to catch on to that. If you put the patient first and focus on what's in their best interest, the profits will come.

Remember, your vision, mission, and core values can (and should) also guide you here. These will serve as an extra filter to help you make sound financial decisions. For example, if your vision is to travel the world with your family, then spending money on a trip to Australia might be a sound financial decision. Buying a Jet Ski, even if it does look *really fun*, might not be.

It just comes down to being intentional. Concrete.

Spiritual Health

I believe that we're all spiritual beings. Body, mind, and spirit. The spirit is something that you need to acknowledge and engage with for your overall well-being. So if you're a Christian, make sure you're engaging in Christian spirituality. If you're not part of organized religion but feel closest to a higher power when you're in nature, then make time to be in the outdoors. If you're Jewish, schedule time off from your practice for holidays. If you're Muslim, schedule your appointments to make time for prayer. Whatever it is that helps you feel closer to your spiritual connection with a higher power, make that element a priority in your daily life.

If you're skeptical of this, consider that research has consistently shown there are tangible benefits to engaging with your spiritual side. Studies from institutions like Harvard and the Mayo Clinic have found that people who actively practice spirituality experience lower rates of depression and anxiety, better physical health outcomes, and significantly higher levels of productivity and job satisfaction. Maintaining your spiritual health isn't just good for your soul; it's good for your practice too.

My one piece of advice here is that there's a difference between people who use spiritually as their identity and those who intentionally practice it. If you say, "I'm a Christian," but never participate in that religion, you're not engaging with the spiritual side of yourself. The purpose of spirituality is for it to be an element of who you are and how you live your life. How you go about that is up to you, but it should be intentional, like everything else we're discussing.

Making Your Life Concrete

Now that you understand the importance of being concrete with your physical, mental, financial, and spiritual health, it's time to take an honest look at where you currently stand. The assessment below will help you identify areas that need attention and guide you toward making intentional improvements.

I use this questionnaire with my clients to establish a baseline and track progress over time. Think of it like taking X-rays with a new patient—you need that initial set of images to properly diagnose and treat. The goal isn't to get perfect scores across the board. Rather, it's to highlight the areas where small, intentional changes could have the biggest impact on your overall well-being and the success of your practice.

Take a few minutes to rate yourself honestly on each item using the 0-4 scale provided. Don't overthink it—go with your first instinct. Once you've completed the assessment, calculate your scores in each category. These scores will help you prioritize which aspects of your foundation need the most attention. Remember, you don't need to tackle everything at once. Pick one or two areas to focus on initially and build from there.

THE CONCRETE LIFE ASSESSMENT

Please answer the following questions on a scale of 0-4.

0: Never 1: Rarely 2: Sometimes 3: Often 4: Almost always

Personal Physical Health

1. How often do you get at least 7 hours of restful sleep per night?
   0 1 2 3 4
2. How often do you engage in moderate to vigorous exercise for at least 30 minutes 5 days per week?
   0 1 2 3 4
3. How often do you consume a balanced diet with fruits, vegetables, and whole grains?
   0 1 2 3 4
4. How often do you avoid sugary drinks and snacks?
   0 1 2 3 4
5. How often do you feel physically energetic and healthy?
   0 1 2 3 4
6. How frequently do you drink less than the NHS weekly recommendations? NHS recommends fewer than 14 drinks/week for men and 7 drinks/week for women.
   0 1 2 3 4
7. How often are you able to spend at least 3 hours outside per week?
   0 1 2 3 4

Mental Health

1. How often do you feel motivated and focused on your daily tasks?
   0 1 2 3 4
2. How often do you manage negative feelings like frustration, anger, sadness, anxiety, or hurt in a healthy way?
   0 1 2 3 4
3. How often are you able to turn negative thoughts around and preserve a positive mood?
   0 1 2 3 4

4. How often do you take time to relax and de-stress and feel refreshed?

0 1 2 3 4

5. How often are you motivated to do the things you know bring you joy and fulfillment?

0 1 2 3 4

6. How often do you feel hopeful about the future?

0 1 2 3 4

Personal Finances and Wealth

1. How often do you keep your emergency savings accounts full or replenish them first when used?

0 1 2 3 4

2. Do you contribute to and fully fund your tax-advantaged retirement accounts?

0 1 2 3 4

3. How often do you set aside funds for specific goals, like vacations or big purchases?

0 1 2 3 4

4. Do you review and update your financial plan semiannually?

0 1 2 3 4

5. How confident do you feel about your debt and strategy for repayment?

0 1 2 3 4

6. How often do you feel confident in your financial stability?

0 1 2 3 4

7. How confident are you in your financial advisor team to look out for your best interest?

0 1 2 3 4

Spiritual Health

1. How often do you spend time in activities that enhance your spirituality (e.g., prayer, meditation, reading spiritual texts)?

0 1 2 3 4

2. How often do you engage in practices that align with your spiritual beliefs?

0 1 2 3 4

3. How often do you reflect on your spiritual growth and personal values?

0 1 2 3 4

4. How often do you spend time with individuals or groups that help you pursue your spiritual health?

0 1 2 3 4

5. How often do you feel a sense of spiritual fulfillment and peace?

0 1 2 3 4

Scoring:

Physical: ___/28
Mental: ___/20
Financial: ___/28
Spiritual: ___/24

Give yourself a grade out of 100: ___

Now that you've completed the assessment, you should have a clear picture of your current foundation. Just like concrete needs the right mix of ingredients in the right proportions, you need balance across these four key areas to build a stable foundation for your practice and life. Don't let a low score discourage you—this assessment isn't about judgment. It's about awareness and intentional improvement.

From here, you can start to use the DRI framework to make incremental changes. Define which areas need the most attention, refine your approach by creating specific action steps, and implement those changes gradually. The key is to start small. Pick the one or two areas where you scored lowest and focus there first.

Maybe it's getting more sleep, starting an exercise routine, or scheduling regular time for spiritual practice.

I've noticed a pattern with my clients where sleep and exercise are often the first things that fall by the wayside. If that resonates with you, those might be good places to start. But you know yourself best—choose the areas where improvement would have the biggest impact on your overall well-being. Whatever you choose, focus on moving one step at a time—from a zero to a one, then from a one to a two.

One final note: If completing this assessment brought up significant concerns about your mental health or substance use, please know that seeking professional help isn't just okay—it's essential. I care deeply about this because I've been there myself. If you're struggling with depression, anxiety, or thoughts of self-harm, I'd once again urge you to pause and reach out to a mental health professional. The rest of this book will still be here when you're ready.

In the next chapter, we'll build on this foundation as we start exploring how to create the practice of your dreams. But remember, everything we cover from this point forward depends on having a solid foundation. Be concrete. Be intentional. The time you invest in yourself now will pay dividends throughout your career.

Define, Refine, Implement

Define: Identify your strengths and weaknesses in relation to the concrete life. Where are you doing well and where are you not?

Refine: Lean into the areas where you're strong and look for ways to improve the areas where you're weak. Come up with a plan. If you're in pain, find a physical therapist. If you're facing financial challenges, find a financial advisor. You get the idea.

Implement: Intentionally *do it*—take the steps to live the concrete life. Commit to yourself and stick with it. Remember that small incremental improvements are the way forward, not changing your entire life overnight.

PERMISSION GRANTED

In the previous chapters, our focus was on setting the foundation for your ideal life. Let's recap:

- You've identified your vision, mission, and core values.
- You've started your blueprint.
- You've made your life concrete.

Now that you've taken those key steps in your personal life, it's time to shift gears and focus on your business. Just like we identified a vision for your ideal life, we're now going to identify a vision for your practice and factor that into your blueprint. And as we make that shift from personal to business, I'd like to introduce you to one simple concept: *The role of the practice is to serve the dentist.*

At a fundamental level, the role of your practice is to serve you. Yes, your practice can and will help people. Yes, there's more to it than just you. But when it comes down to it, your practice is the vessel that will help you achieve your life's vision. And if you want to achieve that vision, you must accept this fact.

Adopting this mindset can be challenging because of the conditioning we've received as healthcare providers, but hear me out. I believe we all find fulfillment from providing a great team environment where our employees thrive and provide excellent care for our patients. That's why we're in this business in the first place—to care for people. But too often we do this to our own detriment. My argument is that the practice needs to be run in a way that provides the dentist the best life possible so they can continue to provide the best experience for their team and patients throughout their entire career. When you think about it that way, you can see how this mindset actually benefits you *and* your patients.

It's Your Practice

Like you, I was conditioned to endure suffering. It's a requirement to become a dentist. From an early time in our education, we realized that we'd need to sacrifice significant time and money to become a doctor. For most of us, this began in high school. I know it did for me.

I was a three-sport varsity athlete and team captain, served in my church, and worked hard at AP classes to distinguish myself from my peers while holding a few different part-time jobs (including making and installing tombstones—a story for another day). While friends were at the mountains skiing or the lake wakeboarding, I was working, practicing, or studying. The same pattern repeated itself in college.

In college, as I mentioned in the introduction, I took a full course load and worked full time. My evenings were split between studying for engineering tests and making recruiting calls to my peers. The goal was seventy-five calls per night. In between classes, I was holding interviews or cold-calling another professor to allow me to speak for five minutes to their class about the internship. I spent the spring and summer coaching my team on how to run painting businesses and regularly logged fifty to sixty hours per week building that business to be top-five in the nation. The conditioning to endure suffering continued into applying dental school. Get good-enough grades, score high enough on the DAT, volunteer, be a leader, and then ... once you've cleared those hurdles ... it's time for actual dental school.

Long hours and daily hazing by grumpy old dentists mixed with the competitiveness of dental school is more of the same. Just a bit more sacrifice till we get that doctorate. Just a thousand more late nights and long weekends dedicated to pursuing our goals. Work hard for your goals and jump through a seemingly endless array of hoops in the hopes of becoming a dentist one day and being in control of your future. Congratulations, Doctor! You're now an associate dentist.

My experience as an associate was like that of a lot of dentists: Do what you're told, use this material, and make sure the big cases go to the owner. Or maybe it was working for a big chain, and it was even worse. You have no control of your schedule, unreasonable expectations of production, and the numbers you're supposed to hit are seemingly impossible. Just a bit more sacrifice and "putting in your time," and you'll reach the pinnacle of your career: practice ownership.

This was my path, and unfortunately I couldn't shake that mentality of self-sacrifice when I started my own practice. I was conditioned to do everything for everyone else. I created a practice that put me last. From working late hours, including Fridays with no vacations to creating very flexible payment terms for patients, I'd inadvertently built the final hoop to jump through on the way to dental burnout. I'd created my own suffering.

I began to ask myself, "Is this all dentistry has to offer me?" "Now what?" and "What am I missing?" It started to make sense why dental schools are run by grumpy dentists. But I knew there were plenty of doctors out there that didn't feel the way I did; who didn't have dental practices that were running them into the ground. That's when I realized that the only way for me to keep myself motivated and stay positive in dentistry was to take charge of my practice and build it into what I'd dreamed about. *I didn't need anyone's permission!* There are no more hoops to jump through, tests to pass, faculty to please, or bosses to tell me how to be a dentist. I own this business. I'm a healthcare entrepreneur, and I can do what I want!

This brings us to a crucial mindset shift many owner-dentists struggle with: seeing yourself as "just a dentist." I've found that most dentists identify first and foremost as dentists—it's their primary identity, with business ownership being secondary. But I approach it differently. I see myself first as an entrepreneur and businessman who happens to have a dental degree. This shift in perspective—from "I'm a dentist who owns a business" to "I'm an entrepreneur who practices dentistry"—can transform how you approach practice ownership. When you identify primarily as a business owner and entrepreneur, you naturally take more control and make decisions that serve your vision rather than letting the practice control you.

This was a massive paradigm shift for me. The long hours, long weeks, and stressful weekends were no longer necessary. It was time to shape my practice into what I'd dreamed about a decade prior when I made the call to become a dentist. It was time to fight for the dental practice that I *wanted* and not what my patients, my team, or my vendors said it should be. Understanding that I'm in control and that my practice needs to be designed around serving *me* first was an epiphany that I'm grateful for. I realized that until I'm truly fulfilled as the owner of my business, I can't fully give to my team and patients. If my practice is running *me*, then I'll end up burnt out, unmotivated, and unable to be a great leader or a compassionate care provider.

In our family, we talk about things that "fill our bucket." What gives you joy and fills you with energy? What activities do you do (or used to do that you need to revisit) that leave you with more energy, joy, excitement, or vigor? At that point in my career, all I could tell you about was what "emptied my bucket." Long hours, stressful patients, an extra beer to help with anxiety, and no time off. In the time since, I first changed the focus of my life, then designed the practice around that.

What fills my bucket? I love to spend time with my wife and my kids. I love to exercise—*a lot*. I crave adventure and new experiences. My wife and I want to travel to all corners of the globe and experience as many cultures as possible. In my previous life, those activities remained a dream. They were things we talked about but never did—habits I wanted to form but found excuses to avoid. This was a big moment when *define, refine, and implement* made its greatest impact.

My wife and I revisited our goals and dreams for our life, our marriage, and our family. Once we had a clear vision, we looked at what the business needed to be to support that. If I was going to be able to be home more with the energy required to be a present father, then I'd need to get home before 5:00 p.m. We changed our practice hours to support that goal. If we were going to travel internationally at least once per year, I needed to be able to take two weeks off in a row during the kids' summer break. So we changed our vacation policy at the office. If I was going to exercise the way I really wanted, I needed to quit drinking and create a routine in my life that allowed for ten hours of exercise per week.

Some of these changes were drastic. I told my team we were changing the hours and days that we worked. We went from working 8:00 a.m. to 8:00 p.m. Monday through Friday to 8:00 a.m. to 4:00 p.m. Monday through Thursday. We removed three individuals and a third-party service. I didn't ask for anyone's permission. During the meeting where I announced this to my team, I did listen to concerns and addressed them as best as possible. The biggest concern was their pay. "Will I still make the same amount as I did before?" was asked the most, which made sense. Whenever there's a change, your team wants to know if they'll be safe. It's your responsibility to offer reassurance that they are. (And their pay stayed the same, just to be clear.)

Afterward, they were all invited to speak to me individually as well. A few of the changes were gradual. The vacation policy and scheduling took about a year to iron out. My morning routine took some time as well. Leading during transition is a challenge, but having a well-thought-out vision and mission that's routinely communicated will offer assurance and stability for you and your team to create a business that supports you first so that you can support your team and patients to the best of your ability for the length of your career. Remember the decision-making framework we discussed in chapter 1? The same concept applies here—whenever you're making big changes, asking yourself, "Is this in line with my vision, mission, and core values?" should help ensure you're making the right decision.

My hope is that you will take time to define what you want in your life and career. Let this vision guide you in refining where you are by adding to it what brings you joy and removing the elements that leave you feeling empty. You're capable of creating a great life and using your business as a healthcare entrepreneur to support it. Make the changes you want and make them when you want. Permission granted.

Reconnecting with Your Passions

I'd guess that you probably had a few things you were *really* into as a child. Maybe one of them was a sport. Maybe one was a hobby like playing guitar or drawing. The kind of things you couldn't wait to do when you got home from school, that you did for fun and nothing else. I'd also be willing to wager that you don't spend much time on those things anymore—maybe ever. Why is that?

I know how it goes. Life got busy, dental school made it impossible, and these days you're just too exhausted to prioritize those things. Learning how to play the piano doesn't seem like a top priority when you're trying to make ends meet in your business. I can't tell you how many dentists I've heard say the phrase, "I used to really enjoy . . ." as they think back fondly on their college baseball career or that time they played in a rock band.

Used to? Why? *You don't need permission to do things you enjoy.*

In fact, you should be *prioritizing* those things. You're in a unique position as a business owner in that you have complete control of your time. Want to join a recreational baseball team, but they only play on Thursday afternoons? Guess what, your office is now closed on Thursday afternoons. *You can do that.*

And you know what makes this even better? When you were a kid, you couldn't afford to buy that new bike, new guitar, new *whatever* you wanted so badly. Now you can, and you don't need permission from anyone to do it. (Note: Author assumes no responsibility for any subsequent marital disputes over your vintage guitar collection or life-size Star Wars AT-AT purchase.) We only have one life to live, and while I do find my dental practice fulfilling, I don't want to spend all day every day in it. That's why I've set my hours accordingly: I don't work on Fridays, and I take seven weeks of vacation every year to do the things I love, like signing up for the national championship mountain bike race in the Swiss Alps (on accident and a story for another time) and going fishing with my friends.

This stuff is important. When you're working on that back lower molar, and the patient's got a big tongue, and you can't see half of what you're trying to do, having something to look forward to, knowing that life's not just a drag, and that you've got your passions and hobbies—that's a huge motivation. It makes going through harder things easier, knowing you can reconnect with those things that you love.

I work with a dentist who loves Legos. Ever since he was a kid, he's loved building with Legos, and he's a pediatric dentist, so he made the decision to design his practice around them. He has Legos in his waiting room; he has Lego-themed artwork on the walls; he even has models on display that he built himself! How awesome is that? Another dentist I work with loves dance and theater but wrote these passions off after starting her own practice, as they no longer fit with her schedule. Eventually, after some prodding, she called me up and told me how she changed her hours so that she could act in a play at her local theater.

Even for me to write this book, I had to make some changes at my practice. I normally take lunch from 12:00 to 1:00 p.m., but the writing program I was working within had calls on Wednesdays from 11:00 a.m. to 12:00 p.m. Writing this book was important to me, so I shifted my lunch an hour earlier to be on those calls, meaning my team had to reschedule six months of patients. That's four patients, four times per month, over the course of six months—eighty-four patients overall. So my team had to call each one and say, "Hey, sorry, I know we've had this scheduled for months, but we need to change it now."

Was it inconvenient? Yep. But guess what? Nothing caught on fire, no one came for my head, and my practice is doing just fine. Even if that cost me a patient, it was worth it because this book is important to me. It's something I wanted to do.

Now, let me be clear. For most entrepreneurs, shifting their schedule is no big deal. For dentists and doctors, it is. You have a team of people and an entire population of patients that are scheduled out months in advance. I understand that this is scary. It might feel unrealistic. But you *can* make these changes, and the world won't come crashing down. People may disagree with you. They may not like it. But it doesn't matter because it's *your* business and you can do what you want with it. Taking time for yourself and prioritizing your own well-being makes you a better practitioner, a better boss, a better leader, and a better person.

If you want to take a dance class, but it's only offered from 2:00 to 4:00 p.m. on a Thursday? Guess what, you close at 2:00 on Thursdays now. Why? Because you said so. Because you will be more fulfilled in your life. You'll be a better parent, a better boss, and a better doctor for doing this. Because you're living your best life, and in the end, everyone will benefit from this decision, even though it might be slightly inconvenient.

So now that we've gotten that out of the way, let's talk about making this happen.

Creating Your Practice Foundation

It's time to sit down and define the future you want to build with your practice, just like you did with your personal life. Luckily for you, it's essentially the same process—creating a vision, mission, and core values for your practice will give you and your team some much-needed clarity and direction. If you happened to skip the first chapter, now would be a good time to go back and familiarize yourself with personal vision, mission, and core values. Since I'm assuming you already have a general understanding of these concepts, I'm going to skip the basics and get right into how to think about them for your practice. Also, your personal mission, vision, and core values will dictate what you do here—so it's the best place to start!

There's one obvious difference between what we did in chapter 1 and what we're doing here, though, which is that you're now involving more people—your team, primarily, but also your patients and the community you're in. Think of this as a collaborative exercise that starts with you. It's your practice, after all, so you have the ultimate say, and you should be setting that direction. But since this will affect other people, you'll want to get feedback from your team. You want them to have a stake in this so it doesn't feel as if they're simply following your lead. Remember, you're a leader—not a dictator!

> **TIP:** If you get overly negative feedback from your team when you first present your vision, vmission, and core values, that's likely a sign those employees are not a good fit for your business. This is your practice! You set the tone. While you should welcome constructive criticism, unconstructive or extreme criticism is a red flag—for them, not you.

Practice Vision

Your practice vision is specific to what you want your practice to represent. Like your personal vision, it's forward-looking and aspirational. I define practice vision as *a clear, concise statement describing what a dental practice aims to represent and become, serving as its aspirational destination.* This vision establishes the practice's ultimate purpose and desired reputation. It's about what you and your team are trying to become. What you want to be known for. The long-term impact you want to make. What you stand for.

Many companies have wildly aspirational visions around changing the world or helping millions of people. SpaceX's vision statement, for example, is "to enable humans to become a multi-planetary species."[v] Microsoft's vision statement is "to help people and businesses throughout the world realize their full potential."[vi]

The problem with these statements is that they're too big to dictate daily behavior. It's also impossible to know if they've been achieved or even if progress has been made toward them. Especially for a smaller business like yours, it's much more valuable to have a specific vision statement that's attainable on a daily basis. That way, you'll always know when you're moving in the right direction.

My practice vision: "Everyone who interacts with Thrive Family Dental is treated with love, dignity, and respect." This encompasses everything I want my practice to be known for. It's what is most important to us above all else. It's simple, clear, concise, and it's something that everyone at my practice can strive to achieve on a daily basis. If we all treat people with love, dignity, and respect, we're on the right track. We're following our blueprint.

You also might have noticed that this doesn't just apply to my patients—it applies to *everyone who interacts with Thrive Family Dental.* That was a very specific choice because I want my team, vendors, partners, and everyone that interacts with my practice to feel that same level of love, dignity, and respect. I'd suggest thinking the same way for your practice vision.

One important note before we move into implementation is that your practice vision should ultimately come from you. When we get to core values, you'll see that I recommend working through those with your team. Your practice's vision is just too close to you to include others. So I recommend doing this exercise on your own and sharing the vision with your team once you've solidified it. Again, the role of the practice is to serve the dentist—and just like your personal vision dictates the future of your life, your practice vision dictates the future of your practice. That's a decision that should come from you and no one else.

Practice Vision Exercise

One exercise I like to go through with my clients is to write their ideal five-star Google review. Your ideal review would dictate how you want people to think about your practice. Based on how we just defined your practice vision, it's a great way to quickly clarify what's most important. And the best part is that this comes fairly naturally—it's not an exhaustive exercise that will take hours of introspection.

You're welcome to just start writing and see what comes up, or you could look at your current five-star reviews to see what's resonating with you. Maybe you already have one review that's just absolutely perfect in your eyes. Great! Use that!

However, if you'd like some guidance, here are a few questions to consider when thinking through this exercise:

- What would you want your clients to say about their experience at your physical practice?
- How would you want them to feel after leaving?
- How would you want them to think about your practice's role in the community?
- How would they compare you to other dentists they've worked with?
- What unique differentiators would they see in your practice?

- What caused them to go out of their way to write this review in the first place?

The idea is to work through this exercise and then distill the primary sentiments of that review into one clear, concise statement that everyone in your practice can easily commit to memory. When I did this for my practice, I found that I kept coming back to the way people felt after coming to Thrive Family Dental. I wanted them to not just feel like they got a great cleaning, but also that they were treated well, made comfortable, and felt at home with us. The last thing I would ever want is for someone to leave an appointment feeling like they weren't heard, that they were talked down to, or that they were uncomfortable. So I distilled this sentiment into my current practice vision: **Everyone who interacts with Thrive Family Dental is treated with love, dignity, and respect.**

Practice Mission

If you start looking at other companies' visions and missions, you'll often find some overlap. It can be hard to distinguish between a vision and a mission, and there are plenty of companies that use the terms interchangeably, or have a vision that looks more like a mission and vice versa.

That might be okay for them, but for our purposes, there's one key difference between the two. Your vision is the "what," while your mission is the "how." Your vision should be forward-looking and aspirational, whereas your mission is what you're doing every day to achieve that vision. It's important to have both because your vision helps with long-term decision-making and strategy, whereas your mission helps you with more short-term and day-to-day decisions. And as long as your vision and mission follow those general guidelines, you'll be set up for success.

I define the practice mission as *a statement outlining the specific actions and methods a dental practice uses to achieve its vision on a daily basis.* Put simply, your mission is what you're doing now to achieve your vision. It should be memorable, specific, and help guide both short-term and day-to-day decisions. To get you thinking, here's my practice's mission:

> **Thrive Family Dental is passionately committed to the mission of restoration. Our primary goal is to restore patients to their optimal oral health, ensuring they can smile with confidence. We are dedicated to restoring the trust of patients in their dentist, providing a transparent and compassionate service. We strive to restore a positive and uplifting work environment, where our team can thrive and provide the best care. Lastly, we are devoted to restoring our community to the way it was designed, contributing to its well-being and prosperity through our actions and services.**

The concept of "restoration" became central to our mission after several years of practicing dentistry and reflecting on what truly made our practice exceptional. In talking with my team, we noticed that all our most impactful work centered around restoration in different forms. It also aligns closely with my Christian faith, as Christ's mission was to restore the broken relationship between humanity and God. As a Christian, I'm called to help restore God's kingdom on earth as it was originally intended, hence "restoring our community to the way it was designed."

At the most basic level, we restore broken teeth and help our patients restore their optimal oral wellness. But really, it runs even deeper—we restore patients' trust in dentistry after negative past experiences where they may have felt unheard or experienced pain. That's why our mission statement breaks "restoration" down into four clear categories:

1. Restoring patients to their optimal oral health
2. Restoring the trust of patients in their dentist

3. Restoring a positive and uplifting work environment
4. Restoring our community to the way it was designed and contributing to its well-being

This mission provides a comprehensive overview of what we're doing at Thrive Family Dental on a daily basis. The vast majority of our efforts and actions are focused on one of those four components of restoration. When we're making business decisions, it's easy to ask ourselves, "Will this help us in our mission of restoration?"—whether related to oral health, trust, work environment, or community. If the answer is yes, then that's a sign we're moving in the right direction.

Your mission doesn't need to have four components. It could have one; it could have five. I'd recommend keeping it relatively concise, though. Remember that all this should be memorable. It's not just going to be written on a whiteboard somewhere or listed on your practice's about page. Your practice's vision, mission, and core values should live inside the heads of your employees. Everyone should be able to recite them from memory. Only when that is achieved will you actually realize the value of these tools.

I'd also recommend avoiding clichés. Something like "We're on a mission to change oral health and patient-dentist relationships" might sound great, but it isn't useful on a daily basis. Specificity is key!

Practice Mission Exercise

Following is a step-by-step exercise that I've used with my clients to help them build their mission statements. Once again, we're going to use the DRI framework to think about this carefully, ensuring the final mission statement is aligned with our goals and will accomplish what we want it to accomplish.

STEP 1: DEFINE

Clarify the reason your practice exists and what makes it unique. This becomes your *purpose statement*, which is your starting point.

Your Purpose:

- Why did you choose to open/buy and lead this dental practice?
- What impact do you want to make in your community?
- What drives you to serve your patients every day?

Example Purpose Statements:

- "To provide high-quality, gentle dental care that helps patients achieve lifelong oral health."
- "To create a welcoming, judgment-free environment where patients feel valued and cared for."

Write your purpose in one clear sentence: _____
_____
_____

STEP 2: REFINE

Think about the audience you serve and your long-term goals. These details will bring focus and direction to your mission statement.

Your Audience:

- Who are your patients? Families? Professionals? Individuals with dental anxiety?
- What do they value when choosing a dental practice?
- How do you want them to feel when they walk through your doors?

Your Long-Term Goals:

- Where do you see your practice in five, ten, or twenty years?
- How do you want to be known in your community?

Examples of Goals:

- "To become the most trusted dental provider in the local area."
- "To redefine the dental experience by blending innovation and personalized care."

Write two to three key audience characteristics: _____
_____
_____
_____

Write one to two long-term goals: _____
_____
_____
_____

STEP 3: IMPLEMENT

Now, combine your purpose, audience, and goals into one powerful, concise mission statement. Aim for the following:

- **Clarity:** Simple, clear language.
- **Brevity:** One to two sentences that are easy to remember.
- **Inspiration:** A statement that motivates your team and connects with your patients.

Example Mission Statements:

1. "To provide exceptional, compassionate dental care while creating a comfortable and welcoming environment for every patient."
2. "Our mission is to deliver personalized, state-of-the-art dental care with integrity and excellence, helping every patient achieve a healthy, confident smile."

Write your final mission statement: _____
_____
_____

Practice Core Values

Just as they did on the personal side, your practice mission and core values operate in tandem. Your mission is what you and your team are doing now to achieve your vision, and your core values are the guidelines that dictate your collective behavior.

One way to think of your practice core values is as "nonnegotiables" for your work environment. These are the qualities that you look for in an ideal employee—and conversely, if an employee was missing one of them, it would cause problems. It's also worth remembering that it's *your practice*, and once again, you have full control over this. You don't need to follow what you've seen others do or what "looks good on paper." These core values will dictate how your team operates and what it's like to work at your practice on a daily basis, so act accordingly.

As an example, here are my practice's core values:

1. **Have Fun:** Work every day with a positive attitude to foster a fun environment to be in.
2. **All Hands on Deck:** Everyone will help anyone when it benefits the practice or the patients.
3. **Never Stop Learning:** Embrace new ideas, grow as an employee, and look for innovations.
4. **Go the Extra Mile:** Find ways to create unexpected service and experiences for our patients and our team.
5. **Be Supportive:** Use empathy and compassion to meet patients and team members where they are.

Let's quickly take a closer look at these so you can see exactly why we've chosen them and how they fit into the daily lives of our employees.

"Have fun" is something I'm obviously not willing to compromise on. After the initial experience I had running my practice, I don't ever want to dread coming to work—and I don't want my employees to, either. I want my dental practice to be fun, positive, and enjoyable to work in for everyone on my team. So I simply ask that we all prioritize being positive and cultivate a fun work environment. We all have to be here eight hours a day; we might as well make the most of it.

"All hands on deck" is originally a sailing term. On a sailing vessel, there are normally three eight-hour shifts. So when you're working, someone else with your same role is off-duty or sleeping, and vice versa—allowing the boat to function twenty-four hours per day. An "all hands on deck" moment is when the ship is in peril due to a storm or something, and everyone has to come on deck to help, regardless of whether they're on or off duty. In my practice, this is simply a mentality of stepping up and doing whatever you can when the time calls for it, even if it might be outside your role.

This is something I learned by trial and error. Within dentistry and in other areas of my life, I've worked with people who have a very narrow focus on their role and nothing else. Toilet's clogged? *Not my job.* Phone's ringing and the receptionist isn't around? *I don't answer phones.* Fridge needs to be cleaned? *Someone else will do it.* I can't stand this type of behavior, which is why one of our core values is "all hands on deck."

"Never stop learning" is fairly self-explanatory. I'm the type of person that wants to be continually learning and growing, so I want to surround myself with people who have that same mindset. As an employer, I want my employees to be eager and excited about learning new things. The last thing I'd want is for an employee to get annoyed or frustrated when I try to teach them something new. So it's a core value.

"Go the extra mile" and *"be supportive"* are both directly in line

with our practice's vision and mission. If we want to achieve our mission of restoration, I need a team that's willing to go the extra mile and find ways to deliver unparalleled service to our patients. And similarly, if everyone who interacts with Thrive Family Dental is to be treated with love, dignity, and respect, then I need a team that's supportive and compassionate with both patients and team members alike.

This is how I want my team to operate. These core values are not just about creating a successful practice—they're about creating *my ideal practice*. And yours should be too.

Practice Core Values Exercise

Developing your practice's core values should be a collaborative effort. That's why I recommend scheduling a meeting with your team solely focused on discussing your core values as a group. The idea is for everyone to think about their own core values, then share them with the group to see what commonalities arise.

The interesting thing about core values is that for the most part, they're already ingrained in your team. Whenever you get a group of people together, there will be customs and norms—this exercise is designed to identify the positive ones that you want to continue to emphasize and integrate into your practice. It's not like you're just coming up with these things out of thin air; more like looking back at how you've already been operating and identifying what you want to prioritize moving forward.

Here's an agenda for how I recommend running that meeting. One important note is that you should also be completing this exercise alongside your team.

Core Values Meeting Agenda:

Step 1: Ask everyone to think about a time or situation when they felt they were serving at their best, creating impact, or enacting their core values. Have them write it down.

Step 2: Have everyone summarize their story in five words or fewer.

Step 3: Ask your team to share their stories. See what commonalities arise. Discuss any insights that may occur. Write down the shared sentiments on a white board or piece of paper. *(Note: Do not share your story first! Whatever you say will have an effect on their stories. Your job here is to simply inquire and appreciate—but don't add. Thank your team for sharing, and then you can share your story at the end if you'd like.)*

Step 4: Repeat the above steps three to five times to generate more shared sentiments.

Step 5: Ask everyone to write down their top three to five core values of what's been generated.

Step 6: Ask everyone to write down some ways they can continue to demonstrate and uphold those core values in their daily work.

Step 7: Share your findings, write down any commonalities, and collect the work from your team.

This exercise can take some time, but it's important to trust in the process and go through it step-by-step. By the end, you'll have a comprehensive list of what your team considers their best core values—and I can practically guarantee that there will be some obvious commonalities. Those commonalities then become candidates for your practice core values, which you have the ultimate say over.

For example, when I did this exercise, my team and I all shared similar stories of going above and beyond when it came to meeting our patients' needs. For years, we'd been doing things like buying flowers for our patients when a family member dies, sending them care packages when they're going through a rough time, and identifying ways to make their experience in our practice more comfortable. It became very apparent that "Go the extra mile" was one of our shared core values because we had been expressing it for years, and we all loved operating in that way. So "go the extra mile" is now listed as one of our core values.

One thing to keep in mind during this exercise is that you can dictate or influence many of these core values. I'm not saying you should manipulate your team into doing exactly what you want, but since you're completing the exercise alongside them, you have an opportunity to bring up what you're thinking and gauge your team's response. When I did this exercise, I already had a good idea of what I wanted to express in my practice's core values. So when it came time for me to share, I emphasized the elements I wanted and used those to guide the group (sometimes literally, by choosing to write or not write on the whiteboard). This isn't nefarious. This is your responsibility as the leader of your organization—to guide your team in this process of creating your core values in a way that's aligned with your vision and mission. What gets included in your practice's core values is ultimately your decision.

That's also why the last step of the exercise is for you to take all that information and distill it down into what *you* believe is most applicable or valuable for your practice. Those become your finalized core values.

> **TIP:** I've included a template for this exercise which you can use with your team on drbenfriberg.com/bookresources. In our mastermind, we also do this exercise as a group—it can be helpful to get some outside perspective from fellow dentists! This can be challenging to do on your own, so if you're finding you need more support, just reach out.

Vision, Mission, and Core Values Examples

Let's look at some examples to see how different dentists have crafted their own unique vision, mission, and core values for their practices. These are real examples from real dentists in my mastermind group, and you'll see how they don't necessarily follow the exact same format. That's okay! You should feel free to construct these in a way that works for you and your team.

Example I: John

John (or Johnny, as I know him) leads a well-established pediatric dental practice in Maine that has served his community for over four decades. He took over the practice from his father several years ago and has been working to both modernize its systems and turn it into *his* vision of an ideal practice. That, of course, started with clarifying his vision, mission, and core values—something we worked on together. One thing I love about this example is that John has incorporated his love of sailing into his core values and really made them his own by providing definitions and a boating-related catchphrase for each one. He's also done some awesome branding work to give his practice a more nautical feel—both digitally and in his physical office—which is really starting to make it feel more like *his* practice rather than his father's!

Vision: To become the highest quality, most sought after, exceptional pediatric dental practice in the state of Maine, bringing joy and healthy smiles to children through kindness, integrity, and humility.

Mission: To bring high-quality, comprehensive, and accessible dental care to Maine children, and do it with love, compassion, and empathy.

Core Values:

1. Joy (fun, enthusiasm, positive attitude): *The thrill of heeling over as your sails fill and your speed picks up!*
2. Teamwork and collaboration (support, energy): *All hands on deck!*

3. Kindness (compassion, empathy): *Selflessly helping another dock their boat in heavy winds!*
4. Perseverance (persistence, tenacity, determination, dedication/commitment to task/goal/our mission): *Weathering the storm!*
5. Coachability (communication, gaining/seeking knowledge, improvement): *Sailing requires skill, knowledge, and attention to safety... effective communication with your crew is essential!*
6. Striving for excellence (be the best we can be, professional growth, always be prepared): *Achieving maximum hull speed, hoist the main!*

Example 2: Richard

Richard purchased an established practice two and a half years ago in Idaho, after working as a traveling dentist performing specialty procedures across the country. Coming from a military background, he's transformed what was previously an insurance-driven practice into a more comprehensive care model focused on full-mouth reconstruction and cosmetic dentistry. I met Richard at a conference in Cleveland after a previous consulting group's attempt to take him out-of-network left him struggling financially with little guidance. Through our work together, he's developed systems to successfully transition away from insurance, become a better leader, and build his practice in a way that's aligned with his vision, mission, and core values.

Vision: To be the premier North Idaho dental practice that positively impacts people's lives. We strive to treat each person with love and kindness and communicate with them in a way that makes them feel special. We believe we can change lives by changing smiles and improve overall health and well-being.

Mission: To create an exceptional experience by building trust and confidence through extraordinary care.

Core Values:

1. Love
2. Service
3. Teamwork
4. Communication
5. Integrity

Sharing with Your Team

Once you've clarified your practice's vision, mission, and core values, the next step is to get them off the page and into your team's heads. I can't emphasize how important this is. If these things just live on a piece of paper locked away in a file cabinet in some storage closet somewhere, you might as well not even bother. So there are two elements to consider here: 1) sharing them with your team for the first time, and 2) ensuring they live in your team's heads and are practiced daily.

Once you've finalized all three components on your end, I recommend sharing them with your team in a meeting. This is an important meeting, and not one I can easily tell you how to run through on these pages. Keep in mind that most people are very resistant to change. You're now coming to your team and saying, "Hey, this is the new direction for our entire business. This is how we're operating." In some cases, this might be a very minor change. In others, it could be significant. There are a lot of leadership elements that go into how you convey that message, some of which we'll cover when we talk about your leadership philosophy.

If you're struggling with how to approach this meeting, reach out to me via DrBenFriberg.com—this is something we talk about in-depth in our mastermind. The important thing is to make sure your team understands the significance of these three things. This isn't just something that can go in one ear and out the other; it's something that will be ever-present in your practice from that point forward. If there are going to be significant changes that come as a result of your vision, mission, and core values, then you'll need to be careful about how you approach that. No change happens overnight, so be sure to remind your team that this will be something that happens gradually over time (even if you'd like to flip a switch and have everyone change their behavior the next day).

After that meeting, there are a bunch of ways you can ensure your team not only retains this information but uses it to dictate their behavior on a daily basis. Throughout the book, I'll be mentioning situations where these come up, like in our morning huddles when we each choose one core value to focus on that day. But some more pointed recommendations include the following:

- **Make them visible:** Write your vision, mission, and core values on the whiteboard in the break room. Maybe you want to paint your vision on a wall in your practice. Maybe you want to create some posters for people to put at their desk. Anything to keep this stuff visible and top of mind.
- **Bring them up:** As the leader, part of your job is to now reinforce your practice's vision, mission, and core values with your team. Your goal should be to bring this stuff up so often that your team is rolling their eyes at you.
- **Add them to your hiring process:** We'll talk more about this later, but the vision, mission, and core values of your practice should be included on every job description. Bring it up in your interviews. You may even want to ask new hires to memorize them.
- **Use them to answer questions:** This is a great one. When someone on your team asks you a question, you can use your vision, mission, and core values to help them find the answer themselves. Respond by asking them the question: "What do you think the answer is, given our vision, mission, and core values?" Over time, they'll learn to use that as a filter before bringing questions to you.

Leadership Philosophy

Everything we've covered up to this point is going to be instrumental in building your seven-figure practice. Your vision, mission, and core values are the blueprint that will help you build your ideal practice—but they'll only work if you understand how to lead your team. Without the right leadership skills, none of this will come to fruition. I'm sure by now you're clear on that, considering we're halfway through the leadership part of this book—but I'll take any chance I get to reinforce this pivotal mindset.

Leadership can mean different things to different people. So before we get into the "how," let's clarify the "what." What is leadership? My definition for leadership is this: *modeling personal values, motivating others with clear purpose and vision, and driving the team to achieve the mission and improve the organization.*

But that's just *my* definition. And I make that clarification because I'm a firm believer in developing your own *leadership philosophy*—the first step of which is to create your own definition of leadership. You know how everyone has a different learning style? Some people are visual learners, others are auditory, and so on? Leadership is kind of similar. Everyone has a slightly different leadership style, and one isn't necessarily better or worse than the other. There are essential leadership skills that every good leader must have, but there's also more than one way to fill a tooth. Good leaders understand how they like to lead and communicate that to their team.

In comes your leadership philosophy. This is an outline of how you choose to interact with your team and what they can expect from you as a leader. It should be written down and shared with your team so everyone is on the same page. This document will ultimately dictate how you run your practice.

I developed my leadership philosophy after reading a book called *The Leader's Compass* by Ed Ruggero. His process helped me create a document that now serves as my leadership philosophy, which follows.

My Leadership Philosophy

Definition of Leadership: The process of modeling personal values and influencing and energizing people—by providing purpose, vision, direction, and motivation—while operating to accomplish the mission and improving the organization.

My personal leadership philosophy is based on the leadership example of Jesus Christ. My goals as a leader are as follows:

- I will treat everyone around me with love, dignity, and respect
- I will push people to be the best version of themselves in and out of our work environment
- I will be patient with training and building up employees.
- I will consistently applaud and recognize the efforts of those around me
- I will listen to feedback
- I will be quick to apologize and seek reconciliation when I make mistakes or mistreat someone
- I will be proactive in creating a fun and positive work environment
- I will act with integrity and honesty and follow through with my word

I Inspire and Expect from the Team:

- **Good Communication**
    - Speak to each other and about each other in a way that is in line with our vision
    - Speak up if you see a problem and be part of the solution
    - Speak up if you make a mistake—own it and be proactive in fixing it
    - Let the team know when you are not at 100 percent

- o Resolve conflicts immediately and with professionalism
- **Constant Growth**
    - o Set goals for professional and personal growth and meet them
    - o Look for, and accept, challenges that push you
    - o Always look to learn something new to add to the team
    - o Continually pursue spiritual, mental, and physical well-being
    - o Never make the same mistake twice
- **Enduring Integrity**
    - o Do what you say you are going to do—every time
    - o Act ethically and morally in all dealings
    - o Be consistent
- **A Positive Environment**
    - o Show up each day with a great attitude toward achieving the vision
    - o Maintain an all-hands-on-deck work ethic—everyone helps everyone
    - o Own your responsibility to build and protect our awesome company culture
    - o Recognize the efforts of our team and make it known
- **Punctuality**
    - o Be on time
    - o If you are clocked in, you are working
    - o Clock out before you hang out
- **Cleanliness**
    - o Keep your workspace organized, clean, and neat
    - o Keep the office clean—if you notice it isn't, it's your responsibility to clean it
    - o Dress appropriately, professionally
    - o Practice proper hygiene and maintain a presentable appearance every day

Nonnegotiables:
- **Deceit, Dishonesty, Disrespect (a.k.a. the quickest way to get fired)**
    o Lying is a violation of my trust and will lead to a quick release from employment
    o If you fail to uphold our practice vision you will no longer be a team member
    o Stealing is a massive violation and will result in prosecution
    o Hiding mistakes or problems will undermine all our efforts
- **Negativity**
    o Life is hard and your attitude shouldn't make it harder for those around you
    o Pessimism is viral and unacceptable
    o Rumors, gossip, and speaking badly about anyone has no place
    o Complacency is unacceptable

It is my mission to make Thrive Family Dental a safe and enjoyable place to work. We will strive together in an open and honest environment to improve each other and the patient experience daily. If I fail to uphold my philosophy, I will humbly accept feedback and correct my behavior to be in line with what I have promised.

As you can see, this thing goes pretty deep. This isn't a time for vague generalities or high-level thinking—the more nitty-gritty, the better. If you'll indulge me for a moment: Think back on some of the jobs you had before you became a dentist, even if it was a summer job as a lifeguard, waiter, or something like that. Imagine if your manager had given you a document like this on day one. How would that have made you feel about them? How would it have impacted the way you worked? Or the way you interacted with them?

My leadership philosophy is an encapsulation of who I am as a leader. It's me. What you see on the page is what you get. When I hire a new employee, I give them this document, and they know exactly how I'll be interacting with them. They know what to expect, and they also will be able to tell when I'm operating in ways that are out of line with my leadership philosophy. They *also* know that "I will listen to feedback" and "I will be quick to apologize and seek reconciliation when I make mistakes or mistreat someone." So, if I were to operate in a way that's out of line with this document, they should feel comfortable bringing that up to me, knowing that I'll listen to their feedback and apologize if I was in the wrong.

If you like this template, use it. If you feel things are missing, add them! If you'd like to do it a different way, fine. This is your document, and it's your leadership philosophy—make it work for you. The important part is that you write down how you want to lead, how you like to communicate, and what you expect from the people you work with. When I've helped my clients through this process, the answers came naturally for most of them. You likely know these things intrinsically, you've just never taken the time to write them down. So if you're feeling hesitant, I'd urge you to just get started—you might be surprised at how quickly these things come to you, and the idea of everyone understanding you at such a deep level can be pretty exciting.

One final note is that your leadership philosophy can, and likely will, change over time. Think of this as a living document that you can go back and update as needed. If you run into an issue with a team member, think about how you might prevent that in the future—that then becomes a new addition to your leadership philosophy. This could be as small as "It really bothers me when people leave empty coffee cups in the sink instead of just putting them in the dishwasher" or as big as "Stealing from the practice will result in prosecution." It's entirely up to you and what you deem important.

Psychological Safety

I could talk for days about why a clear leadership philosophy is so important to running a successful practice (or any business, for that matter), but if I were to boil it down to one thing, it's psychological safety. Perhaps the most important aspect of being a great leader is creating *psychological safety* among your team. There's even research to back up this claim.

If you're new to this term, *Harvard Business Review* defines psychological safety as "a shared belief held by members of a team that it's OK to take risks, to express their ideas and concerns, to speak up with questions, and to admit mistakes—all without fear of negative consequences."[vii] This isn't something that's related to business, either. It's that same feeling you get when you're with your family or close friends and you know you can be yourself without fear of judgment. When you know that any mistakes or vulnerabilities you exhibit will be accepted and understood. Where you can be fully authentic and self-expressed.

That's not something found in most work environments, and especially most manager-employee relationships. Again, if you think back to previous jobs you've had, chances are you didn't feel this way at work—and certainly not when you first started. Yet research has shown that psychological safety is actually one of the greatest levers for improving team performance.

In 2012, Google set out to understand what makes teams successful with an initiative called Project Aristotle. Their research team spent two years studying 250 attributes of the 180 teams within their company and initially identified four factors of a successful team: dependability, structure and clarity, meaning, and impact. The teams that were performing well had all those four attributes, but there was still something separating the good teams from the great.

That "something," they eventually discovered, was psychological safety. The teams who performed at the highest levels felt safe taking risks and being vulnerable in front of each other. These teams had an environment focused on value and respect, where people felt they could speak up, share ideas, challenge ideas, and express concern without fear of embarrassment or humiliation. In the same *Harvard Business Review* article, Amy Edmondson, a professor of leadership and management at Harvard Business School, remarked, "What they had discovered was that even the extremely smart, high-powered employees at Google needed a psychologically safe work environment to contribute the talents they had to offer."

This was a massive discovery and ultimately changed the way Google, and much of the management world, operated. But don't think this only applies to tech companies. Creating an environment of psychological safety in your practice will make *everything* better—your performance, your team culture, your revenue, your patient experience. Ensuring people feel safe to speak up and share ideas is part of your responsibility as a leader.

Sharing your leadership philosophy with your team is the best way to begin cultivating that sense of psychological safety. (That is, assuming your leadership philosophy encourages people to be open, vulnerable, and share ideas without fear of judgment—which it absolutely should.) When someone reads that document, it immediately creates psychological safety because they know they're working with someone who values them and what they have to contribute. They know they can speak up without being reprimanded. They know they can be themselves.

> **TIP:** When your team comes to you with a suggestion, whether you implement it or not doesn't matter. What matters is that you hear it and consider it. When you do this, you're showing them that you value their input. After listening, you can then use your own filter to decide whether to make that change or not.

This is so important because there are a million things going on in your business that you're not aware of or that you don't interact with. If your team feels like their contributions matter and they know their voices will be heard, they'll speak up about things that aren't working. Or they'll identify ways to improve a process entirely on their own. Or they'll come to you with an idea on how to make patients feel more comfortable.

And here's the best part: When you combine this with your vision, mission, and core values, everything starts to fall into place. Because now your team members are going to speak up when something isn't aligned with your practice's blueprint. Or when they have an idea that would further your mission. Or when someone else on the team isn't operating within your core values.

I don't know about you, but that's exactly how I want my team to be operating. It's not only going to benefit your practice—it will benefit your team's mental health and well-being. Instead of going into work in fear of what their boss is going to say or worrying about making mistakes or lying in bed at night wondering if their boss is mad at them, they can come to work knowing they are valued, safe to be themselves, and that they're contributing to something bigger than their role.

So if you're thinking this stuff isn't important or you can just skip it and get right to implementing some marketing hacks—think again. Leadership will make or break your business, and it starts with you. The good news is that by following the leadership guidance I've laid out here and throughout the book, your business isn't going to break; it's only going to get better.

Define, Refine, Implement

Define: Define and write down your vision, mission, core values, and leadership philosophy.

Refine: Share these with your team and adjust as you see fit.

Implement: Make them visible in your practice and create opportunities during team meetings to remind your team of the vision, mission, core values. Reward those who exemplify them in the practice.

TEAM CULTURE

Can you think back to a time when you were part of a group or team that had a great culture? Where you belonged to a positive group of people that seemed to communicate without talking, encouraged each other, and pushed toward a common goal in unison? For me, it's the time I've spent working with Ideal Practices—a dental consulting firm that helps dentists start the practice of their dreams. (If you're going to do a start-up, they should be your first call.) I've been part of their organization for over five years now and have served as their marketing and "give process" consultant. I currently operate as the director of Mastery Elite, their invitation-only mastermind group.

The leadership team and employees at Ideal Practices are clearly unified by a common vision, mission, and set of core values. When we get together for team meetings or mastermind summits, everything seems to click into place. As an entirely remote team, the principles from the last chapter guide us and create a special environment where everyone is on the same page. We'll go six months without seeing each other and then, over the course of a three-day weekend, create a transformational experience for doctors that are just starting their dental practice from scratch. It really is an amazing experience, and I'm thankful to be part of a team with such a great culture.

At a high level, "culture" is the type of music, food, art, decorations, language, and interactions that certain groups of people have normalized at a societal level. In your business, you'll have a *team culture*—a way of interacting and acting outwardly toward others that's normalized among your group of employees. Team culture occurs any time a group of people get together. There are rituals, rights, actions, and behaviors that naturally establish themselves and become consistent among that group. This is consistent with any group, whether it's a group of friends, family, a sports team, a club—and of course, a workplace.

The reality is, while cultures do form organically, great cultures typically don't appear out of thin air. The reason Ideal Practices has such an amazing culture is because of the leadership skills of their executive team. It's something they've intentionally created. And as a leader, you have an opportunity to do the same thing.

In fact, I'd say you have a sacred responsibility to build a positive team culture in your workplace. If you believe everybody in your practice is only there to serve you and make you money, you're not only hurting your employees—you're hurting yourself and the trajectory of your business. Culture affects everything, and it's not just about making people feel good or being a nice boss. You can't have a seven-figure practice with a negative team culture. End of story.

I first truly realized the relationship between my team's culture and the performance of my practice when I started tracking and analyzing our Google reviews. We're going to go deeper on key performance indicators (KPIs) in chapter 7, but for now, just know that a KPI is a metric used to gauge performance. Google reviews are just one of many KPIs we track at Thrive Family Dental. The idea is simple: If the frequency of five-star reviews goes up, we know we're improving. If it goes down, we know there's something wrong. And at the time of this writing, I'm proud to say we currently have more five-star reviews than any other solo dentist in our region.

The first major correlation I saw when I started analyzing this data was that any time we were having cultural problems in the office, the number of five-star reviews per week went down. Then, after I took corrective action, that number went back up. That corrective action was sometimes as simple as asking my team, "Hey, what's going on? Is everything okay?", in which case I typically found out there was something happening that I wasn't privy to. In some cases, it meant letting someone go—or as I say, making them available to the free market economy to find a culture that fit them.

And here's the crazy thing. Every time I've let someone go because of a bad culture fit, we've had double or triple the amount of five-star reviews within the next few weeks. I remember one time, we went over two weeks without a five-star review—which is very rare for our practice—when I had someone that I knew I needed to let go. We ended up letting them go, and the next day we had three five-star reviews.

This isn't some crazy coincidence or one-off situation—it's happened multiple times. Even though our team has to work harder to overcome the lack of help from that missing employee, everything improves. Our morale, our patient care, our interactions, and the positivity within our team and our patients increases to a point where there's a significant and measurable difference in our five-star reviews.

The moral of the story? Team culture is important. If you think you don't need to be prioritizing culture because your time would be better spent on "revenue-generating" activities, think again. Developing a positive team culture *is a revenue-generating activity*, and it will make your life and the lives of your employees so much more enjoyable. It's *your* responsibility to build it.

Their Best Life

Beyond the revenue implications, part of your sacred responsibility as a leader is to help your employees live their best life. Your goal should always be to create and preserve a work environment where your team can become the best versions of themselves. There are a few areas that have been repeatedly shown to improve job satisfaction—focusing on these will help you create that environment, allowing your team to live their best life in and out of the office. I've distilled the most important elements into the acronym THRIVE. This will help you understand the needs of your team, create opportunities to improve job satisfaction, and continue to create the team culture that you want.

THRIVE: Triumph, Happiness, Relationships, Involvement, Vitality, Enjoyment

1. **Triumph:** Your team wants to be a part of something bigger than themselves. They desire to feel accomplished. Celebrate achievements, both big and small. Whether it's mastering a new technique, growing the practice, or receiving positive feedback from patients, recognizing accomplishments fuels motivation and job satisfaction. Typically, this is going to take the form of verbal recognition, but you can get creative with how you celebrate achievements. In my practice, for example, I buy my entire team a brand-new pair of Nikes for every 100 five-star reviews we generate. Last month, we hit 800, so they've all been walking around in their new Nikes at work. As an added benefit, this often starts conversations with our patients, who are now more likely to give a five-star review once they know it will help the team get to their next pair of shoes!
2. **Happiness:** Encourage your team to start each day with a smile and a positive mindset. This is a muscle that needs to be exercised. Happiness is the foundation of a joyful workplace.

When your team experiences joy, gratitude, and optimism, it creates a vibrant atmosphere that boosts morale and job satisfaction. Think of it as giving everyone a daily dose of sunshine, even on the cloudiest days. As the leader, you set the tone. On hard mornings when nothing feels like it's going right, I sit in my truck in the parking lot for a few minutes and manufacture a positive attitude. It's your responsibility to choose a positive attitude. Your team and patients deserve your best, and you must set the intention every day to give it to them.

> **TIP:** Did you know that around 80 percent of our thoughts are negative? Human beings have a negativity bias that originally helped us survive, but it no longer serves us. When I say, "Manufacture a positive attitude," I mean intentionally ignoring negativity and choosing to focus on the positive. This is in your control. Don't let negative thoughts dominate your life!

3. **Relationships:** Emphasize the importance of building strong, positive relationships within the team. Work becomes much more enjoyable when everyone gets along and supports each other. Encourage a culture where colleagues feel like a winning team, creating a supportive network that makes coming to work feel like the first practice of the year. One of the ways we do this is by dedicating time in our morning huddle for anyone to speak up if they're not feeling 100 percent. They might not feel well, they might be going through something at home—whatever it is, we want to know so we can pick up any slack they might have and support them throughout the day. It's a small gesture that shows we all have each other's backs.
4. **Involvement:** Foster an environment where your team members feel their contributions have meaningful impact. Your practice needs to be a place where employees know their input is valued and considered in key decisions. They should feel empowered to influence positive change, both in how the practice operates and in patient-care outcomes. When team

members understand that they aren't just going through the motions but are truly shaping the direction of the practice, they develop a deeper sense of purpose and satisfaction in their work. This level of genuine involvement creates a more engaged team that takes pride in advancing the practice's mission. In later chapters, we'll cover multiple techniques to make this happen.

5. **Vitality:** Promote a healthy work-life balance and overall well-being. Encourage your team to take breaks, stay active, and prioritize their health. When your team feels physically and mentally energized, they're more likely to be productive and satisfied with their work. It's like having a team of superheroes, ready to tackle any challenge with vigor and enthusiasm. This starts with you by working toward an inspirational lifestyle that your team wants to engage in as well.

6. **Enjoyment:** Create a fun and enjoyable work environment. Organize team-building activities, celebrate milestones, and inject a bit of humor into the daily routine. When your team enjoys coming to work, it creates a positive atmosphere that enhances job satisfaction. It's like adding a sprinkle of joy to each workday, making it a place where everyone looks forward to being.

The six elements of THRIVE are ultimately the key to creating a positive and fulfilling work environment for your team, which then extends to everything else in your business. A happy team leads to happy patients and a thriving practice!

By the way, did you notice how "money" isn't included in any of these? That's because money is actually fairly low on the list of factors for job satisfaction. Depending on which survey you're looking at, you might find slightly different results, but things like meaningful work, recognition, appreciation, work-life balance, and good relationships with coworkers are nearly always above compensation.

Here's a list of the top ten factors for job satisfaction according to a Boston Consulting Group Study that surveyed 200,000 employees:

1. Appreciation for your work
2. Good relationships with colleagues
3. Good work-life balance
4. Good relationships with superiors
5. Company's financial stability
6. Learning and career development
7. Job security
8. Attractive fixed salary
9. Interesting job content
10. Company values[viii]

Money is a minimum level of motivation, meaning you need to pay someone X number of dollars to live, come to work, and trade their time for money. But once they've received that, a little bit more or even a lot more doesn't increase job satisfaction or motivation.

There are too many employers who think, "Well, I pay them, therefore they should be [insert positive quality here]." That's simply not the case. Just because you're paying your employees—even if you're paying them exceptionally well—does not guarantee they'll be productive, motivated, or happy in their roles. Put simply, if money is the sole motivator for your employees, you'll receive the bare minimum of performance in return. Each employee will have their own motivations, and it's your job as a leader to understand those and adapt yourself and your practice to ensure you're meeting them.

What do your employees really want to get out of their time working with you? What do they want to achieve in their careers? In their home life? You'll never know the answers to these questions until you start asking them. The jobs of an office administrator, dental assistant, or dental hygienist are career-specific, each with their own skill sets and standards. Just like you wanted to improve your skill sets and climb the next ladder rung in your career, so do they.

The fundamental principle here is just to be a caring person. If you don't care about your employees having the best life possible and you don't take that responsibility seriously, you'll never have a positive team culture. Your business *will* suffer as a result. When you care about your team, and they see it every day, they'll care about their jobs and the impact they're making on your business. They'll want to help you build a better practice.

Positive vs. Negative Team Cultures

So, we've already clarified that "team culture" occurs naturally any time you get a group of people together—there will always be rituals, rights, actions, and behaviors that establish themselves over time. Sometimes these behaviors are positive, but sometimes they're not. Ultimately, it's your responsibility as the leader to ensure your team's culture is trending in the positive direction.

A *positive team culture* is one where everybody comes together and builds each other up in pursuit of a common goal. When they go home, they have more energy. They've got energy for their spouse, their kids, their community, and positivity grows. This ripples out to affect nearly every facet of your business. It creates better patient experiences, increases employee retention, and leads to meaningful growth. It's a net positive.

On the flip side, a *negative team culture* can be toxic, impacting patient care and making your own life miserable as the practice owner. If your employees go to work, and it's all negative, they're going to have less energy for their family when they get home. They won't want to put their best foot forward at work, and they won't have a desire to grow inside your business. It's a net negative. This often leads to poor productivity and high turnover. If you can't seem to motivate your team consistently, and you're constantly needing to hire new people, that's a sign you have a negative culture.

One of the reasons I feel so strongly about this "sacred responsibility" to create a positive work environment is because we don't know what happens to our employees when they leave. We don't have control over what happens to them outside of work, but we do have control over what happens during the workday. We can use that time to create a net positive or net negative impact on their lives—and that's a serious responsibility. In chapter 1, we discussed how your actions outside of work affect your performance at work. Well, this applies to your employees, too, and it goes both ways. Their work environment affects their lives outside of work and vice versa.

If one of my team members is a parent, for example, the way they interact with their children is impacted by the way I interact with them. So I have a responsibility not only to that person, but to those children as well.

One of the greatest compliments I've received was from the husband of one of my employees who came to me and said, "It's like I have my wife back. The last office where she worked, she would come home miserable. They took everything they could from her and gave her nothing. Now, she comes home with a smile. She's energetic and happy. I can't tell you how much that means to our family." That's the type of impact you can have as a leader.

And let's be clear—culture isn't just about having a foosball table in the break room or celebrating birthdays (although those things can be part of it). Culture is about the underlying values, beliefs, and behaviors that drive your team's interactions and decisions every day. And it starts with the leader. Part of your responsibility in creating that positive work environment is to lift people up, encourage them, support them, and empower them in their roles (we'll talk about more specifics on how to do this soon).

Another key part of that responsibility is what type of behavior you permit. It takes everyone on the team to create a great culture, but it takes only one person to destroy it. Your team culture is largely defined by the worst behavior you permit. I've had owner-dentists come to me and blame their negative culture on one "toxic" person. But really, this is just a sign they've failed as a leader. As the leader, you are responsible for creating a standard, calling people to that standard, then giving them opportunities to correct if they aren't able to meet it. If you hold up your end of the bargain, and still, after multiple correction opportunities, they aren't meeting the standard, you've hired the wrong person, and it's time to make them available to the free market economy.

Which does beg the question: How can you hire the right people from the beginning to avoid those problems before they occur? Your mind is in the right place—incorporating team culture into your hiring process is the best way to get things moving in the right direction. Let's see how that works.

It Starts at Hiring

Ask any successful entrepreneur, and they'll tell you they'd rather hire someone with less experience who's a good culture fit than a highly experienced person who isn't. Why? Because you can train skills, but you can't train culture. When I'm interviewing, I tell every prospect the same thing: "I rabidly defend my company culture because I'm the only one who has to work here. Everybody else chooses to."

In my practice, you don't get to come into the office in a crappy mood and sulk through the morning huddle. That's not who we are. You either need to tell us what's going on so we can be supportive and understand why you're upset, or you need to manufacture a positive attitude. I'm not going to let whatever you've got going on pull the whole team down. What we're trying to accomplish is hard enough.

This is entirely in your control as the practice owner. Your culture is what you want it to be—that's it. For example, I'm a dog person. We have a dog in our office named MEADOW who is part of our team. (And no, I'm not yelling at you—her name is in all caps to delineate between a dog and person in text. This is a requirement by Paws4People, an organization we've partnered with that you'll learn more about in future chapters.)

MEADOW wears a uniform, she's on our website, and she interacts with my patients on a daily basis. She has over two years of training and helps our patients who suffer from dental anxiety or fear by sitting in their laps while they get the treatment they need. I love MEADOW, my family loves MEADOW, our team loves

MEADOW, and our patients love MEADOW. She's a very positive part of our team culture.

I don't hire cat people. That might sound a little ridiculous, but guess what? It's my practice, and I know that cat people are not going to be a good fit for my business and my team culture because we're all dog people. If I don't want to hire cat people, I don't have to hire cat people. That's okay. It's your responsibility as a leader to clarify what it means to be a good culture fit for *your* business, then use the interview process to determine whether a prospective hire fits what you're looking for.

The best way to do this is to make sure you're asking culture-based questions in your hiring process. You can develop these from your practice vision, mission, and core values—below, I've shared a few examples of how I've done that in my own business. Even if you're not currently hiring in your business, I'd prioritize updating your interview process so you'll be prepared for the next round of hiring. This shouldn't take long.

Culture-Based Interview Questions

I already mentioned that one of our core values is "all hands on deck," which means everybody must be willing to do every job at some point unless a license stops you. So in our interview process, we ask people to tell us about a time they've had to do somebody else's job. If they struggle with it or if they describe a very minor situation, that's a sign this person might not be aligned with our "all hands on deck" core value. Conversely, if they say, "Oh my gosh, it happens all the time!" and start talking about the endless number of times they've jumped in to help their coworkers, that's a great sign for us.

Similarly, one of the defining factors of my practice is that we do same-day dentistry. If you call us with a problem, and we can figure out a way to help you right now, we're going to do it. It's tough and it can be stressful at times, but it's part of our mission of restoring patients to their optimal oral health. We always equate it to a circus act spinning plates—I've got team members holding the sticks, I'm spinning a plate, then they take over, and now we're going to add a whole new plate. It's a very dynamic environment.

There are some employees who are very straight-lined. They think, "This is what we've got planned today, this is what we're going to do today, and that's all we're going to do today." Those employees don't thrive in my practice. They can't be that dynamic. They can't add another spinning plate. They just implode. And here's the thing: *That's okay.* There's nothing wrong with that person! They're just not a good fit for my business. They'll be able to find a job that suits them somewhere else. In fact, I'm doing everyone a favor by not hiring them—they'll be better off, and so will we.

It's important that we set up our interview process to filter out those types of people. So we ask every candidate to tell us about a time they've worked at a practice that had a dynamic schedule. If they say, "I love a dynamic schedule! In the last office where I worked, things were changing all the time—and I loved it!" that's a great sign. And if they say, "The last practice where I worked only saw six patients per day, and we had a policy that said we would only book appointments seven days in advance," that's not a great sign.

I recommend reviewing your interview process with your practice's new core values in mind. You should have at least one question per core value that will tell you whether the job candidate is aligned with your practice. Those questions need to be reflective of

> **TIP:** Once you've asked the question, *stop*. Don't lead them to the answer you want. When I ask people to tell me about a time when they've worked at a practice with a dynamic schedule, that's all I say—I don't explain what a dynamic schedule means to me or the fact that we pride ourselves on doing same-day dentistry. I don't give them any clues as to which way I want them to answer, which means I get a more honest response.

the *behaviors* that reflect your core values.

Hiring the right people from the get-go will make your life significantly easier, but it's by no means a magic pill that will solve all your culture problems. Your work doesn't end after the hiring process—really, it's just beginning. It's your job to lift your employees up to the standard you've set, then help them maintain it. So let's take a look at how that typically works.

Reinforcement through Praise and Correction

We've already clarified that team culture is a set of norms, behaviors, actions, beliefs, and rituals that a group of people share. So your job in maintaining this culture is to reinforce behavior that you want to continue and correct behavior that you don't. Core values are once again the guidelines that will help you do this. And I'll go back to my "all hands on deck" core value to illustrate how this can work in practice.

If the phone is ringing in my practice, answering that phone is a high-value activity. That's a potential new patient or new appointment, and a missed call could mean they go somewhere else or we have to play phone tag getting back to them, and they're starting off with a bad experience. At Thrive Family Dental, our dental assistants and hygienists know that if the administrative team can't get to the phone for whatever reason, it's their responsibility to step up and grab the phone. And not just grab the phone or put them on hold, but to engage with that person and move them toward coming through our doors. They're responsible for performing and providing the best phone call experience they can for our future patients.

This isn't typical in most practices, but it is in mine because "all hands on deck" is one of our core values. That's the mentality, and

I've reinforced this in my team through praise and correction.

When I see a hygienist pick up the phone, I'll walk up to them and say, "Hey, that was really awesome. I saw how you grabbed the phone and got that new patient scheduled. I appreciate that and I'm really grateful. All hands on deck." That positive reinforcement continues to encourage that behavior so that the next time the phone rings, my hygienist is going to be more likely to grab that phone. And yes, I do mention the specific core value when I see it—this is done intentionally, to keep our core values top of mind.

On the other hand, if I notice this isn't happening, I have an opportunity to correct the behavior: "Hey, I saw you were in your operatory, writing your notes for the day, which is awesome, but the phone rang, and you didn't get up to grab it. That patient went to voicemail, and we may not get to schedule them because they might go to a different office. So next time, just make sure if the phone is ringing, you can grab it for me. All hands on deck, right?"

That's how you can use your core values to reinforce the right culture among your team. It's all about reinforcing through praise and correction in an intentional yet polite way. Always remember that tone and body language matter when communicating with your team. In the next chapter, we'll cover more opportunities for this type of connection with one-on-one meetings.

When done correctly and consistently, reinforcement and correction will get you far. If you're having problems with your culture but you're not consistently reinforcing and correcting your team's behavior, you only have yourself to blame. If you're doing this consistently and things still aren't working, that's a clear indicator

> **TIP:** *Praise in public, correct in private.* Praising in public is a great way to boost morale for everyone. Correcting negative behaviors in public, however, is a morale killer. Praising in public encourages the individual because they get recognized in front of their peers, *and* it motivates those who heard the praise. This positive reinforcement means *they're* more likely to exhibit that same behavior in the future.

that someone may not be a good fit for your business and should be made available to the free market economy.

Solidification by Firing

In order to establish the right team culture, you have to be prepared to let people go. Firing is one of the hardest things any employer has to do, especially if they're an empathetic leader who wants the best for their employees. Personally, I can think of many times when I was too reluctant to fire people, and it negatively impacted my team culture. That's something I'm continually trying to improve—being more decisive when it comes to knowing when to let someone go.

The reality is that it takes everyone on your team to create a positive culture, but it only takes one person to ruin it. When someone isn't a good culture fit, it quickly brings the entire team down. That's why team culture should always be a priority when you're looking at whether to keep someone or let them go.

It's amazing to see the difference in a team's performance after removing bad culture fits. They feel better emotionally and have more energy because they don't have that negativity draining on them. It also shows them that you're on their side and that you're a team. The fact that you're willing to go through the entire process of firing someone then recruiting, interviewing, hiring, and training someone new—simply because they weren't a good fit for the team—shows that you value their well-being.

This is ultimately what will preserve the value of your company, your team culture, and your own personal fulfillment. If your team is happy, they'll perform better, and your practice will provide a better experience for you and your patients. For all the pain that firing may cause, that's the upside—and ultimately, it ends up being a net positive in 99.9 percent of situations.

But I understand that making that decision can be challenging. So here are three questions to ask yourself when you're considering letting someone go.

1. Have they been given opportunities to correct their behavior?
I once had to fire a dental assistant because she was, put simply, a toxic employee. She did her job very well, but the way she interacted with my team didn't create a positive work environment. People didn't enjoy coming to work because of her presence. So initially, I'd correct her behaviors that were causing friction in the practice. I sat with her multiple times, mediated conflict between employees, and even brought in a consultant to work on communication styles. Unfortunately, the toxic behavior continued. Eventually, I'd given her enough opportunities to correct that behavior, and she didn't. That was a clear indicator that she wasn't a good cultural fit for our team and had to be let go.

2. Has your team spoken up?
People who feel psychologically safe at their place of work can come to their boss and express problems. That could mean any number of things—a problem with some process in their role, a patient, or most importantly, an issue they're having with a fellow employee. My team knows they can tell me what's going on in the office, and I'll take it seriously. Our vision of love, dignity, and respect is helpful here, as they're unlikely to complain or talk negatively about someone for no reason. That's not aligned with our vision as a practice. And similarly, because they know the importance of our vision, they're likely to mention situations or people who aren't aligned with it.

That means when they do come to me, I take it seriously. And you should too. If someone on my team comes to me and says one of their coworkers is causing problems or other people on the team are having a hard time working with them, it's my duty as a leader to listen to their feedback and address it so we can maintain that positive team culture. When I do this, it also shows my team that I value their input and gives them even more positive reinforcement, showing them they can always come to me with problems.

If you're not getting feedback from your team, that could mean things are going great. It could also mean they don't feel psychologically safe enough to bring issues to you. In either situation, the answer is to communicate with your team and let them know you want to hear about what's going on in the office—good and bad. This is something that can also take place in your one-on-one meetings, which we'll talk about in the next chapter.

3. Are they capable of growth?
This is a more obvious one, but it's worth clarifying the impact it can have on your culture. Your employees need to be able to fulfill the responsibilities in their role. That's a given. But they also need to be able to grow and adapt as your practice changes. They should be ready and willing to learn new things and take on new responsibilities.

I once had an employee who was a great culture fit—she didn't rub anyone the wrong way, she was fun to be around, we all liked her—but she wasn't capable of growth within her skill set. She had multiple opportunities to work on specific step-by-step improvements in her skill set, and there was no growth after six months. The same issues were happening over and over again, and it got to a point where one of her coworkers was taking on a lot of her workload as a result. That person was now dreading coming to work because her workload had nearly doubled, and she had no support. So we had to let the problematic employee go.

This is a perfect example of how team culture and performance are inherently intertwined. It's not one or the other. You need both, and they build on each other. If performance is lacking, culture will take a hit. If culture is lacking, performance will take a hit. As I work with more and more dentists, I continually find that those who support their team from *both* a cultural and performance perspective have the greatest success, fulfillment, and positive work environments.

So, quick recap: You can support your team's culture by hiring correctly, reinforcing positive behavior, correcting negative behavior, and firing bad culture fits once you've exhausted all other options. Those are the primary actions you can take as a leader to influence your team's culture. This next part might be a bit counterintuitive, but there's something to be said for what you *don't* do as a leader. Sometimes, you just need to leave your team alone and trust they'll do things right. Sometimes, you just have to give it up.

Give It Up

You might not like to hear this, but I'm going to say it anyway: *Most dentists are control freaks.* I say this as one myself. The reality is that to excel in a career that requires less than fifty micron margins for crowns to be considered successful, you have to be a bit of a perfectionist. From a clinical perspective, we live in a world of micro control—and because most of us don't have managerial or leadership training, that mindset we've been indoctrinated into often overflows into the way we run our business and lead our team. This then affects culture because, let's be honest, working with a control freak isn't exactly fun. So let's talk about it.

Your employees want to have ownership over their role and build a fulfilling career. What they *don't* want is to be micromanaged by their boss. To achieve the former, they need to have a certain level of autonomy and ownership within their role. This helps them feel like they're making a meaningful difference in your organization—because they are! The problem is that because of our "control freak" nature, we often become obsessed with making sure every little thing is done perfectly—and we inadvertently end up taking away that autonomy and ownership in the process.

This causes problems for the employee, of course, but it's also problematic for the dentist. Many dentists don't fully trust their team, so they feel as if they need to do all the work themselves. That's a surefire way to burn yourself out and sabotage your business. If you're doing everything in your practice, how will you have the time to learn new skills? To take continuing education courses? To spend time with your family? Or to just take a break in between patients to make sure you're operating at your best?

There's a mindset shift that needs to happen here. You're not a dentist who owns a practice; you're a healthcare entrepreneur. And just like an entrepreneur needs to delegate to scale their business, so do you. You've got to figure out how to off-load as much of the burden and responsibility you're facing as possible. Giving up that responsibility can be difficult, but when done incrementally and with the right process, it's incredibly freeing. Work becomes more enjoyable. Your team enjoys work more. You don't end up spiraling and feeling as if everything is always on you.

The golden rule is that if someone can do a task 70 percent as well as you can, it's worth letting them do it so you can continue to focus on what you do—which is dentistry and leadership. The 70 percent rule in delegation is attributed to Jim Schleckser, author of the book *Great CEOs Are Lazy*.

You should also consider the fact that for every task you hate doing, there's someone out there who loves doing it. So part of your job as a leader is to figure out what activities bring your team joy and get them into a position where they can take on that type of work. In many cases, that also means taking something off your plate that you don't like doing. It's a win-win. This is one of the most important lessons any leader has to learn—it will give you more freedom, improve team culture, improve employee retention, and ultimately set your business up for long-term growth.

But when it comes down to it, you need a process to ensure your employees are successful in this. Most of the time, when a dentist comes to me complaining about something they delegated that went wrong, it's not the fault of the employee—it's the fault of the dentist for not giving that employee what they needed to succeed. So when it comes to delegation, there are really four key steps you need to take to ensure things go right.

Step 1: Ensure they *want* to do it.
If I want to delegate a new responsibility or task to one of my employees, I don't simply order them to do it. I first ask them if they want to do it. In the process of asking, I'm offering a "why" I want them to do it and creating a call to action. There's a nuance to this—instead of being told what to do, they're now electing to do it

themselves. By raising their hand and saying yes, they are inherently taking ownership over that task. It's not someone else's job that they have to do—it's theirs. That means they'll feel responsible for it and want to do a good job.

In most cases, I have a specific person in mind who I think would be a good fit for the task. I'll talk to them one-on-one and ask them if they're interested in taking it on. I'm clear on my expectations, and I let them know how I can support them in getting started. In some cases, and especially with less specific tasks, I'll simply pose the question to the entire team: "Hey, who wants to plan the Christmas party?" That's something I'm happy to give to anyone who raises their hand.

Now, what happens if they say no? Well, that's for you to decide. One of our core values is "never stop learning," so my employees are typically eager to take on new responsibilities. There are valid reasons to say no (you're at capacity, it's not in your zone of genius, someone else is better suited to it), but if someone is avoiding taking on additional responsibilities for no other reason than that they "don't want to," that's a red flag.

Step 2: Communicate the *impact* of what they'll be doing.
Once you've had that initial conversation, it's critical that they understand the impact of what they'll be doing. Even if it's something that seems trivial, be sure to give them the bigger picture and show how their actions will affect the practice and the team as a whole. When they understand *why* they're doing it and the impact they're making, they'll be a lot more motivated to do it—and do a good job.

For example, I've completely delegated my organic social media posting. I used to be responsible for it, and it never got done. It's also not in my skill set, so I asked my receptionist if she'd be interested in working on social media. I saw this as a great skill for her to learn that could serve her well in her career, and it would be a huge help to me and the practice.

She was a little hesitant at first, until I communicated the importance of what she'd be doing. I told her, "So, this is something that will really help with patient growth. Patients look at social media to vet their new dentist, so if we have a positive, exciting social media presence, it's going to increase our new patients. They'll trust us more, we'll make more money—it's just a really great addition to our practice and our marketing efforts. What do you think about taking that on? I know you'll do great, and I'll be here to support you. I'm also going to make sure you get some educational resources to help you get up to speed."

Let me tell you, that hesitancy disappeared pretty quickly. She now runs our social media, and I'm completely hands off. It took a little while—in the beginning, I coached her and reviewed all her posts—but now I don't do anything other than hide from her when she's got the camera out.

Step 3: Work with them to create a system on *how* to do it.
You can't expect to delegate something with no instructions and have someone execute it perfectly, just as you would. If you want to successfully delegate a task, you need to spend time documenting the process and creating a system for completing it. You need to walk the employee through it and give them the proper training to ensure they're set up for success. If there are specific ways you want something done, this is your time to show them, like I did with my social media manager. And please don't do this after the fact, when you're frustrated and angry about a mistake they inadvertently made.

The key lesson here is to make sure your employee has everything they need to be successful. I didn't just assume my receptionist would be able to take on our social media accounts with no input from me or no education. I let her know that I'd not only support her myself, but provide her with educational resources to help her. You can—and should—ask them directly if you've given them everything they think they'll need. "Do you feel like you have everything you need to be successful with this?" They should be part of this process, since they're the ones that will be doing the work. We'll touch a lot more on how this all works in part II, when we talk about business systems.

Step 4: *Trust* them to do it correctly.
Once you've taught them how you want it done, you have to give them the freedom to do it on their own. This is where many leaders get it wrong. They hover, they nitpick, they micromanage—no. *Walk away and go do your job while they do theirs.* You can monitor from afar if the situation calls for it, like if it involves a patient or if a mistake could be costly, but for the most part you want to remove yourself to see if they can handle it without you. Let them know you're confident in their abilities and that you want to see them do it on their own before offering any advice: "Okay, I feel good about this. I know you'll do a great job. I'd like you to do the next one on your own, and we'll regroup later to discuss how it went. You can come to me with questions if needed, but I trust your judgment. Sound good?"

Step 5: *Verify* they've done it correctly.
Now that they've finished the task, you can come in and verify that it's been done correctly. This is your chance to educate and offer more training if needed. The more they do it right, the less you have to verify. As that happens, their confidence builds, they feel more fulfilled in their role, and they can see how their contributions matter. They understand that you trust in them to do this task, and you believe in their abilities. That goes a long way.

There's an art to delegation that you will learn over time. These four steps will help you get started. The real key is that you *do* get started. I know from experience that there are often endless excuses for not delegating something: "I need to get my process down first." "I don't know if they're quite ready for this." "I'll do it when I have some spare time." There will never be a perfect time to delegate something, and the longer you hold off, the worse it will get. Trust your team, follow the steps, and get started. I recommend starting with the things you procrastinate on the most. Those are clearly things you don't like doing and are likely not in your unique skill set, so you should prioritize getting them off your plate. Write those down in a list and assign a relevant team member to potentially take them on. Have the conversation.

On the next page, I've included a worksheet to help you get started on this.

My final piece of advice? Don't sweat the little things. Remember the golden rule: If someone else can do it 70 percent as well as you can, then it's worth letting them do it. You don't want to live a life where you're constantly stressed, worried about having to handle everything yourself. Part of building that ideal practice and ideal life is accepting the fact that others may have a different way of working, that mistakes will happen, and that sometimes "good enough" is better than "perfect." It also means accepting the fact that you don't need to make every decision in your business.

Decision Boundaries

Some leaders feel that their job is to make all the decisions in their business. Those leaders aren't very good leaders. Because really, the job of a leader is to educate and empower your team to make the right decisions on their own. While it's true that there are certain decisions only you can make, there are also countless decisions someone else can make. Decisions that don't require your unique expertise—just some logic, a bit of training, and good judgment. All of which are things your team should have in spades!

If you find yourself making all the decisions in your business, or your team is constantly coming to you and asking you how to proceed, that's a problem. Not only is this taking up your valuable time and theirs, it's a clear indicator that you aren't giving your team the autonomy they need to operate effectively in their roles. And when everything has to go through you, you're implying you don't trust their judgment—even if that may not be true.

DRI Delegation Worksheet

Here's a simple list of questions you can ask yourself any time you want to delegate something in your business. Working through these questions in advance ensures there is clarity, accountability, and that your delegated tasks will be completed efficiently.

Define:

- **What task needs to be delegated?** *(Example: Sterilizing instruments, scheduling follow-ups, handling patient intake)*
- **Why is this task important?** *(Example: Ensures patient safety, improves workflow, enhances patient experience)*
- **What is the desired outcome?** *(Example: Instruments are ready before each appointment, appointments are confirmed within twenty-four hours)*

Refine:

- **Who is the best person for this task?** *(Consider skills, availability, and interest)*
- **What resources or training are required?** *(Example: Sterilization protocols, scheduling software tutorial)*
- **What are the specific steps to complete this task?** *(Example: Break the task into manageable steps)*
- **What are the deadlines or checkpoints?** *(Example: Daily, weekly, by the end of each shift)*

Implement:

- **How will the task be communicated to the team member?** *(Example: In a team meeting, through written instructions, or one-on-one)*
- **What tools will you provide for tracking progress?** *(Example: Task lists, software dashboards, or regular check-ins)*
- **How will you measure success?** *(Example: Task completion rates, accuracy, or team feedback)*
- **What follow-up process will you use?** *(Example: Weekly review meetings or immediate feedback after completion)*

The answer to this problem is to set clear boundaries around what decisions have to go through you and what decisions your team can make on their own. These boundaries are typically going to be on a person-to-person or role-to-role basis. Each person on your team should understand when they're allowed to make a decision on their own and when to get you involved.

There are many aspects of my practice that I'm not involved in. For example, I have delegated inventory and ordering to my lead dental assistant. I don't know what she buys or when she buys it. I don't care. But I do know she has a specific set of parameters to work within because we both agreed to them a long time ago. She knows she needs to have a minimum level of inventory on hand so we don't run out of certain supplies and that we keep our supply and material costs below 5 percent of collections. Beyond that, she can make all the decisions. I'm not worried about every nickel and dime we spend on inventory. I don't care what the cost of my air water syringe tips are as long as they fall within our budget. Yes, I could sit down and spend hours obsessively finding the cheapest possible cost for every item we buy, but that would actually be a net negative, as I could be generating more revenue in the business elsewhere.

And beyond the monetary value, I could be spending that time at home with my family. Or learning a new procedure. Or getting to know a colleague. That's more valuable to me than saving eighty-four cents on a bag of cotton rolls. I've set the budget, I've given that responsibility to someone else, and I trust them to make those decisions. I don't stress about it.

Now, the other level of this is that I've educated my team on the decision-making hierarchy for our practice—which is guided by our vision, mission, and core values. The idea is that any time we are considering making a change or adding something new, we ask ourselves three questions:

1. **Will it increase efficiency or profitability?**
2. **Will it improve patient care?**
3. **Will it make our jobs better or easier?**

If it doesn't check at least two out of those three boxes, the answer will probably be no. And because my team is aware of this hierarchy, they can use it as a filter to understand when something is worth bringing to me. A $3,000 automated espresso machine? Yes, it will improve the patient experience, and it will make our lives better and easier by providing great coffee, but is it worth the $3,000 hit to profitability when the Nespresso machine is already working well? Probably not. That's going to be a no.

On the other hand, if someone comes to me and says, "Hey, our scanner is broken, and there's this new one that's way faster. It would cost the same to get this one as it would to repair the old one, and it's going to save us a ton of time!"—that's an obvious yes. Thanks to this decision-making hierarchy, my team is now coming to me with great ideas that will improve our practice, and they're not wasting my time or theirs with ideas that aren't going to move the needle in the way I want.

This combination of delegating and creating decision boundaries is perhaps the number-one most impactful lever in terms of building a seven-figure practice. When people don't have responsibilities or autonomy in their role, when they're forced to do the same thing every day, and they aren't growing in their career—it's demotivating and demoralizing. This is why people look for other opportunities at other practices. The more you lean into delegation, the better everything gets. You become more efficient and effective, patient care improves, morale improves, loyalty and retention of your employees improves. I could go on and on.

Now is a good time to stop and think about your own decision boundaries. I suspect that as you were reading this, you've already thought about what you truly care about and when you do or don't want your team to involve you. Write down your thoughts and turn them into specific boundaries, then share those with your team. This is very similar to the leadership philosophy, as it gives your team clarity on how you want to operate. It's a great tool for everyone involved.

You Can't Skip This

Before we close out the leadership portion of this book, let's take a look back at what we've covered and why it matters. As the owner of a dental practice, you are the leader of your organization—and with that comes a lot of responsibility. You need to learn to lead yourself before you lead others. That starts with crafting your personal vision, mission, and core values. If you haven't already done that, I suggest putting this book down and getting to work. You've already seen how these impact other areas of your business, and that's not stopping any time soon.

In chapter 2, we clarified that you're the foundation of your practice—and just like a building needs a solid foundation if it wants to stand the test of time, your practice does too. Your physical, mental, financial, and spiritual health have a significant effect on the way you show up at work. If you're not intentionally working to maintain those four elements of health, you're missing an opportunity. Another way to think of this is that you have the income potential of a professional athlete. Act accordingly!

Then there's that big mindset shift we covered in chapter 3. You have permission to do whatever you want in your practice. Want to shift your hours? Go for it. Want to reconnect with a long-lost passion? This is the time to do it. You can also use your personal vision, mission, and core values as a starting point to develop your practice's vision, mission, and core values. These will serve as the guardrails that keep your team operating in the right way and your practice moving forward in the way you want. Once again, if you haven't taken the time to create these and write them down, I'd suggest doing that now before you move on.

And finally, we explored team culture: what it is, why it's important, and what you can do to improve it. This stuff does impact your bottom line, and that's really just the beginning. Out of everything we've discussed in this part of the book, team culture is the one that's going to crop up on a daily basis. Reinforcement, correction, hiring, firing, delegation, decision boundaries—these are the things

I wish they taught us in dental school because a good leader relies on them every day.

If it wasn't abundantly clear already, I'll reiterate: *You can't skip this.* The first part of this book is about leadership because it's the number-one skill you need to build a successful practice. Everything else builds on this. You can have the best business systems, KPIs, and marketing strategies in the world—but if you're not leading your team well, it won't get you far.

Great leaders aren't born overnight, but getting all the information is half the battle. You're well on your way, and if you need more assistance or you're unclear on anything we've discussed up to this point, you're welcome to reach out to me at drbenfriberg.com or join me in my mastermind. There's only so much detail I can include in a book, and the mastermind is my way of providing more hands-on help.

And with that, it's time to get into the nitty-gritty elements of running a dental practice: management. This is where it gets sexy!

Define, Refine, Implement

Define: Determine what you want your ideal culture to be.

Refine: Think about what you need to adjust or add to your environment and team to achieve that ideal culture.

Implement: Use THRIVE to ensure you're hitting on all the critical areas of job satisfaction.

Part Two

MANAGEMENT

WHEN TO LEAD AND WHAT TO MANAGE

Before I started my own practice, I worked for a few different dental practices. The journey I took through those workplaces really opened my eyes to how different leadership styles and management strategies affect a practice and the people in it. In fact, those experiences played a huge part in how I now conduct myself as a leader because they showed me firsthand what worked and what didn't. If you're currently working in someone else's practice, keep an eye on what's working and what isn't, what you like, what you don't like, and how certain things affect the team—it will be valuable for you one day as a practice owner. (That knowledge plus what we've covered in this book is going to set you up very, very well.)

For a few years, I worked at a corporate dental chain that had about seventy locations around the country. This place was run like a well-oiled machine—every single thing had a system, and everybody knew what they were supposed to do and when and how they were supposed to do it. They had all the metrics—KPIs of new patients per day, production, collections, accounts receivable, and scoreboards to monitor everything.

On paper the practice was performing well, but in reality things were going downhill. Looking back, I now know that the practice was successful largely due to the efforts of one senior dentist who was the third-highest grossing dentist in the corporation. He was generating more than even the oral surgeons—and he somehow managed to lead the practice through the endless red tape and bureaucracy that was forced on him by the corporation.

When he left the practice (around the same time I did), what little leadership there was left with him. After that, they were quite literally running the practice through micromanagement. No one was tapping into each employee's "why." No one was concerned about their motivations or interested in supporting them in their careers, and it was incredibly demoralizing as an employee. The team had no motivation, no ownership, and nothing keeping them there. They were servants to the corporation and not much more.

The practice soon had a reputation for burning people out—it was like a factory where people would come in, get worked to the bone, and get spat out the other end with nothing to show for it. Turnover was incredibly high, which caused even more problems since they couldn't replace the people who were leaving due to the practice's reputation.

When I left their, I was burnt out on dentistry. I lost confidence in my clinical skills and my treatment planning. The next practice had a completely different approach—and I realized that while I still had all the skills I used to, they'd nearly been managed out of me. I hadn't really been utilizing my skills because I was working in such a highly micromanaged operation. I was just going through the steps of their procedures.

Turns out, they couldn't micromanage their way out of that downward spiral. In 2023, the ownership sold the practice. That came as no surprise to me. You can't run a dental practice (or business, for that matter) on systems alone. You need a combination of leadership and systems.

Ironically, the next practice I joined was almost the exact opposite. It was an independent practice—about as far from corporate as you could get—and the owner was very gregarious. Everybody loved him, and he let his associates (like me) practice dentistry in the way they wanted to practice. I had tons of freedom to do what I wanted and operate in the way I chose. It was kind of a free-for-all.

On the one hand, I had total ownership over the way I operated. It was actually a great introduction to running my own practice, since I was essentially running a small miniature practice of my own inside his. He enabled dentists to do more procedures than other organizations would've. He empowered people to challenge themselves and grow. But under the hood, there were some serious problems. There were little to no systems in place, which meant the patient experience was inconsistent and the team was operating inefficiently. When the owner delegated something (which he did often), there was no support—it was just on you to figure it out.

There were a lot of things I loved about working at that practice. But even with all the benefits, it was hard to ignore the problems. Sometimes it felt like we were running the practice with one arm tied behind our backs because we didn't have the systems or even the physical items we needed. I'm not kidding—there were times we'd run out of inventory because there were no systems in place to keep things stocked. It wasn't a sustainable way of operating.

It was so obvious to me that giving people the freedom to work however they wanted had its perks, but it had plenty of downside, too. And as much as I hated working at that corporate practice, I couldn't ignore the fact that they were at least setting their employees up to operate efficiently. For all the ups and downs I experienced at that point in my life, my time at these two practices taught me a valuable lesson in the difference between leadership and management. And it's one that every business owner needs to understand.

The Difference between Leadership and Management

Leadership and management might go hand in hand, but they're two fundamentally different concepts. One alone isn't sufficient to run an organization—they're both required and must operate in conjunction with one another.

Management is about getting the right things done the right way. It's very much the "how" of running a business. Good management involves creating systems, tracking metrics, documenting processes, and doing all the hands-on stuff required to ensure your team is operating efficiently and producing consistent results. It's about setting up the systems and processes to ensure everything gets done correctly and efficiently. Perhaps most importantly, it's about ensuring things are done the right way every time regardless of which individual is doing it.

That corporate practice where I worked had excellent management. Anyone could come into that practice and perform well because of how well they managed their systems and processes. There was a specific way to do everything. But they lacked leadership.

Leadership is about motivating people to go above and beyond. It's about motivating them to not just follow the systems, but also improve them. To find better ways of working. To go beyond the system and capitalize on opportunities to do better—whether that's making a patient feel more comfortable, saving the business money, or making a coworker's job easier.

The independent practice had (mostly) great leadership. The owner was encouraging, he'd motivate us, and it was a real joy to work there. But they were seriously lacking in management, to the point where it was causing major problems.

There has to be a balance between the two. You won't be able to run a profitable and fulfilling seven-figure practice if your team is operating inefficiently, if your results are wildly inconsistent, or if there are no systems and no ways to track your progress. At the same time, you will not be able to run a seven-figure practice if your team is unmotivated, if they don't want to help your business grow, if they don't see any future growth for themselves, or if they are miserable in their roles.

There's one key takeaway here: *Management ensures a minimum standard of results. Leadership elevates the standard.* Having one isn't sufficient. You need both, and you need to understand when to lead and what to manage.

When to Lead

I know, I know. "But Ben, we just finished the leadership chapters! Won't you give it a rest already?" Just hear me out. Before we dive into management, we have to clarify this difference between leadership and management so you can differentiate between the two. So if you'll indulge me, let's take a quick step back into leadership land before we move on. Just trust me—this is important stuff.

The simple answer to the question of "when to lead" in your business is *all the time*. But when you dig a little deeper, I've found there are really four areas where you need to step up as a leader:

1. **Daily leadership**
2. **Leading through times of change**
3. **Leading through times of crisis**
4. **Forward-thinking leadership**

Daily Leadership

There's no getting around the fact that leadership is required on a daily basis. A huge part of leadership is setting an example for your team by embodying the behaviors you want to see them embody. You can't tell someone to have a great attitude at work and ask them to behave within the vision of your practice if you're not doing the same thing. It's obvious, but it's not always practiced—or not practiced consistently. You have to be the one that sets the example for everyone else. Every day.

My parents used to tell me, "If the leader shows up without socks on, the followers will show up the next day naked." In other words, when the leader exhibits negative behaviors—no matter how small or insignificant—the team will also embody those traits, probably to a bigger, more negative effect. If you half-ass it, everyone around you is going to quarter-ass it. That's why the self-discipline and self-leadership part is so important.

This really comes down to three things: *self-discipline, self-regulation, and self-awareness.* If you can control those three things and people see that, they'll be able to embody that as well. But if you're undisciplined, if you're emotionally dysregulated, if you're not aware of how you're behaving or how your actions are affecting others—that all becomes permissible behavior, and everyone's going to start treating each other that way. I understand that this might sound obvious—it's basically "be a good person"—but when you're dealing with the rigors and stresses of running a business day in and day out, these things can slip. So this is just another area where you need to be intentional. Be concrete.

This type of daily leadership also naturally improves performance. Like I said earlier, leadership is about elevating the standard. Getting the best out of people. Turning your B players into A players.

Leading Through Times of Change

You'll be faced with many times of change in your practice (especially after reading this book!) and these are the moments where you'll really need to step up as a leader. This is when your people will look to you for guidance, direction, and support. How you respond is ultimately going to dictate how you and your team come out on the other side.

Any time you're making changes to your practice, no matter how big or small, it's your job as a leader to think through the "why" behind the change and communicate that to your team. There's a whole science around change management in business, and one thing you'll often hear is that people are very resistant to changing the way they work. While this is true, I think there should be an asterisk there—people only resist changing the way they work *when they don't see how it will benefit them or the business*. When you convey that "why," they see the benefit and go from being resistant to receptive (maybe even excited!) about making the change.

One of my clients experienced this firsthand when they decided to implement a new rule in their practice. The rule was that every new patient would be scanned with a 3D intraoral scanner. From a business perspective, this is a huge win—it gives them better data, allows them to communicate better, and will potentially improve their treatment plan acceptance and increase their case fees. But when the owner-dentist brought this to their team, their hygienists pushed back, saying they didn't have time for that.

Now, realistically, everyone knows that a hygienist has enough time to do a three-minute scan. It adds maybe seven or eight minutes to their procedure time, and their appointment schedule can easily accommodate this. It's a no-brainer. But the hygienists don't want to add this to their plate. Why? Because it makes their lives more difficult, and they don't understand why it needs to happen.

My client had two options here. They could *manage* the situation by saying, "You will do this because I said so, and it is part of your job." Or they could *lead* by explaining how this change affects the goals of the practice and how that extra effort on their part will create a greater impact. My client wasn't sure how to navigate this situation with their team, so I reminded her of how this relates to her practice's vision and how it will benefit everyone as a whole. She then went to her team and said this:

> Look, our vision is to be the best dental provider in our community. We want to be elite. And in order to do that, we need to be able to communicate better than anybody else on the market. We're going to do that through this 3D scanning technology. It's going to enable us to show

patients what's happening with their oral health, meaning we can provide better care. It's going to give us better record keeping. It's going to give us a higher case acceptance rate, and once that starts happening, the practice will grow. And everyone's bonus is based on how well the practice is doing—so in the long run, learning how to squeeze these scans into our procedures is going to make a huge impact for you personally, but also for our patients, our reputation, and our brand. This little bit of extra effort on your part has the potential to make a huge impact and move us closer toward our vision. *Do you think we can figure out a way to work these scans into your schedule?*

See how much of a difference that makes compared to simply telling them they have to do it? It's all about explaining how the change will help accomplish your vision, how it will benefit the team, and how it will benefit the practice. If they don't understand the "why," you're just adding another thing to their plate. When they understand the "why," they're energized and motivated to implement the change because they can see they're making a difference. All that extra effort and hassle becomes worth it because it ladders up to something bigger. They're making a difference. Remember those top ten factors of job satisfaction from chapter 4? This doctor just hit on four points out of the ten—appreciation, career development, interesting job content, and company values.

And did you notice how she asked for their input at the end? That's very intentional, and it's a key part of the process. Asking the team for their input on "how" to implement or accomplish the new task gives them a chance to add their own feedback and provide their own solutions. This does two things: 1) it will likely improve the way the task gets done, since they know more about their role than you do, and 2) it gives them ownership over the situation. When the solution comes from them, they're more likely to do it than when it comes from on high.

> **TIP:** If you do this properly and people are still resistant to the change, that's probably because they're not the right person for the job.

Leading Through Times of Crisis

Times of crisis are when your team needs you most. This is where good leadership can make or break a business. In times of crisis, your team will be feeling scared, nervous, anxious, uncertain, worried—and it's your role as a leader to keep them calm, exude confidence, and bring them through unscathed.

A couple of years ago, I had a water leak in my office. It was over Fourth of July weekend, when everybody was out of town, and it had leaked for three or four days. I was actually heading home from a vacation myself when I got a call from the fire department telling me there was a water main break in my building. I was still about forty minutes away from the office, so I called my office administrator and asked them to go check out what was going on. When they called me back, they told me it wasn't a water main that had broken—it was a tiny little hose that had popped off a piece of equipment and flooded my office. (A piece of equipment I'd personally installed by the way. Yikes!) There was probably a half inch of standing water in about half of my clinic.

Now, we're on the second floor, so you can imagine what happened. There was a dermatology office below us that got partially flooded, which led to a long insurance claim and lawsuit (that's a story for another time). But as I was getting the full damage report over the phone, still on my way to the practice, I knew we had to come up with a plan—fast. There were a lot of unanswered questions. Do we shut down the practice for however long it takes to get everything fixed? What do we tell our patients? How do we reschedule everyone? How do I get my team paid? There were a million questions running through our heads.

To me, the answer was obvious. We had to pack up as much as we could from the office, relocate to a new office, and continue practicing dentistry the next week. As much as it would suck—as much as we all didn't want to do that—it was the best thing for me, the practice, and the team. It was the only way I could keep things moving forward.

This was a moment when I needed to step up as a leader. I had to quickly formulate a plan, communicate that plan to my team, and then take decisive action. That first night, I contacted a few people I knew who had dental space. I reached out to a contractor friend and touched base with my IT company—both of whom agreed to jump in head-first and help me get out of this mess because of the great relationships I'd built with them over the years. So I began to formulate the plan.

On Sunday, I got the team together and said something to this effect:

> Guys, this is a huge challenge for us. This isn't what we expected or wanted, but we're going to get through it. We're going to be fine. Here's what we're going to do: I've already talked to some people, and we are going to move our practice to a different location while our office gets repaired. That means we'll be able to practice dentistry this week, which is going to be the best outcome for our patients, our practice, and for all of us. But it also means that on Monday, we're going to get together and move everything to this new office. It's going to be difficult, but it's not impossible, so let's talk about what we need to do to make that happen.

I then opened up the conversation to all of them, and they stepped up. Together, we planned out everything we'd need to move in order to practice dentistry at that new location, then we banded together to get it done. People were calling patients to reschedule their Monday appointments, people were loading stuff into their SUVs and driving across town—and then we practiced dentistry Tuesday through Friday (instead of our normal Monday through Thursday). We saw a full week of patients and generated the same amount of revenue as if nothing had happened.

Looking back, that crappy situation turned out to be an amazing opportunity for the team to come together and bond over making it through such a difficult shared experience. But it wouldn't have happened without the right leadership. In times of crisis, teams need clear, assertive, decisive communication from their leader. It's your job to guide them through a crisis with a steady hand while offering them the support they need to come out of it unscathed.

This is another example of the DRI framework in action. I *defined* the solution by deciding that we were going to move our office to a new location and continue practicing dentistry the next week. I then *refined* that solution by discussing it with my team and getting their input on what we'd need to move, how we'd move it, and all the other logistics required to make this plan successful. Once that was done, we *implemented* the solution by banding together on Monday and moving everything in one day.

Forward-Thinking Leadership

One of the primary responsibilities of any entrepreneur is to be forward-thinking. If you want to grow your business, move forward, make progress—you have to be thinking years in advance. We've already done part of this by crafting our practice vision and mission. But now, it gets a bit more specific. It's about imagining where you want to be in one, three, five years, then backcasting from there. What are the changes that need to happen to get to that point? What do you need to start doing now to achieve that result? No one else will be thinking this way in your practice. It's up to you.

My practice, has been transitioning from a PPO insurance-driven model to a fee-for-service practice. Obviously, this is a *big* change. It's not something that happens overnight, so I had to be very forward-thinking to start planning and implementing all the changes that would need to take place over the course of years to make this happen.

I started thinking about this change when I was working my butt off, getting home late, drinking too much—that time of my life I mentioned in the introduction. If you have experience with dental insurance and PPOs (which I'm sure you do), then you'll know that you have to do a lot more dentistry to make the same amount of money as a fee-for-service model. The insurance companies are essentially taking a 30 to 40 percent cut of your revenue, which makes for thin margins. The only solution is to simply do more dentistry, and it was causing me and my team to burn out. Now, I'm not saying that insurance is all bad or that every dentist should be moving toward fee-for-service—in chapter 9, we'll talk about how insurance can be an essential marketing tactic for many practices—but for my practice and my goals, it was the best way forward.

So from that moment I described in the introduction, I decided that I wanted to be primarily fee-for-service within the next three to five years. I told my team, and I started to plan out all the changes required to make that happen. We changed our hours to be more conducive to that process. We changed our procedures. I put myself through around 100 hours of continuing education and spent around $70,000 over two years to get myself prepared to be able to provide dentistry at the level required to be fee-for-service. We hired insurance experts and consultants to help us negotiate and navigate going out-of-network in a way that was sustainable for the practice.

And I communicated all this to my team with assertive, clear, decisive communication:

> Over the next two to three years, we're going to pursue a primarily fee-for-service practice. We're going to do it by working with consultants to cancel insurance contracts that don't fit our practice anymore. I'm going to personally improve my skills by attending intensive continuing education courses to be able to do larger cases more often.

Dental assistants, you're going to join me to improve your skills so we can all provide a better level of care for our patients. This is going to be a burden on everyone, but we all have to be in this together as a team. We're going to have to communicate differently. We're going to have relationships that are lost with patients that we love because they're simply not going to go to a dentist who's out of network. It's going to be challenging, but we're going to be so much better off in the end. We're going to work less, take more time off, and make more money. All of us. So, are you on board for this?

Everybody was on board. They knew it was going to be hard, but because I communicated the "why" behind this change, gave them a clear plan, empathized with them, and explained how it would benefit them, they saw the importance of what we were doing.

And it was hard! We had to sit down with patients we'd seen for four years and say, "Hey, by the way, next time you come in, instead of your insurance paying 100 percent of this, they're only going to pay 60 percent. So instead of this being free, it's going to cost you eighty dollars at your next appointment." Our script was deeper than this and talked about the "why" behind this decision and how in the end, it would be a benefit to them as well. (There's an example of this script available at drbenfriberg.com/bookresources.) And we had to hope they valued the relationship with our practice and the care we provided more than their relationship with their insurance company. That's not an easy conversation. But because of all the work we did leading up to that change, we retained a significant portion of our patients. Full disclaimer: We did get yelled at on multiple occasions.

Today, we're only in-network with two insurance companies. We were in-network with thirty-seven. Previously, I would've had to produce $200,000 in dentistry per month to collect $130,000. Now, we produce $150,000 for the same collection. So our profitability is significantly better, and we work less. But that change wouldn't have happened if I hadn't had the vision and forward-thinking leadership to put those changes in place over the course of two years.

(We were also able to make the switch in large part because of our reputation in the community and online. Our Google reviews are off the charts. People are willing to pay out of pocket because we've dedicated ourselves to excellence, and we treat everyone with love, dignity, and respect. That all comes out of what we've covered in parts I and II of this book. It's leadership and management in action.)

What to Manage

Okay—now that we understand when to lead, we can start talking about what to manage. I use the phrase *"what to manage"* because management is more about how the business runs than the people in it. Leadership is people-forward, management is systems-forward.

When I think about management, the main goal is around setting expectations and ensuring consistent performance. This is your job, this is how you do it, this is when you do it, and we're going to hold you accountable to those things. That's management. You can have great morale and motivated people who are working hard, but if they're not doing their clinical notes right, that's a problem—*a management problem*.

Within management, there are two main buckets: human relations (HR) management and business management.

HR management is about ensuring your employees are following the rules and working within the guidelines of the business. This allows for consistency—everyone is doing the right things, in the right way, at the right time to provide a consistent patient experience. There are certain expectations for each role, and the people in those roles need to know those expectations and how to meet them. When a patient comes into Thrive Family Dental for a cleaning, they can expect the same experience every time, regardless of which hygienist is doing the cleaning, because we have systems set up to ensure consistency. Nothing is left to chance.

HR management involves things like job descriptions, SOPs, processes, and training. It's all of the stuff that equips an employee to perform their job correctly, up to the standard you've set.

Business management is higher-level, related to the way the business functions as a whole. There are elements of running a business that you have to manage—accounts payable, accounts receivable, profit margins, budget forecasting, etc. You can't "lead" through these things. This is kind of like Business 101, those core elements of running a business that have to get done correctly. In order to ensure they're done correctly, you need to have the proper systems in place as well as metrics to ensure you're meeting expectations.

We'll get more into those business systems in chapter 6 and metrics in chapter 7, but for now, let's dive a bit deeper into the previous example I gave around how we manage cleanings in our practice. The idea of having a step-by-step process for cleanings isn't exactly novel—I'm sure you're already familiar with this. That said, in my experience, we go a bit further than most with this. At Thrive Family Dental, every step of the cleaning process is documented, from how the hygienist greets the patient to the exact steps they should take to perform the cleaning itself and how the patient's information is logged in our system. At the end of the cleaning, the hygienist is supposed to ask the patient when they'd like to schedule their next cleaning. Every time. That exact question. They then schedule the appointment before they leave the room.

That's correct! The patient doesn't reschedule with our receptionist. In fact, they often don't even need to stop at the front desk on their way out because our hygienists can also handle small payments. They're the one that has spent time with the patient and developed that personal connection, so it only makes sense for them to ask about booking that next appointment.

We then have a KPI called hygiene reappointment percentage. You're probably already aware of this, but for the uninitiated, this KPI tracks how many patients are actually signing up for their next cleaning before they leave our office. Our goal is for 90 percent of patients to book their next cleaning before they leave our office.

That metric, combined with our system for cleanings, is one way we manage the performance of our hygienists. I can look at that KPI for each of our hygienists and see who is performing up to the standard I've set (90 percent). If someone is below 90 percent, it's then my job as a manager to talk to that person. Are they asking the question every time? Are they following the system we have in place? If not, why? Is there maybe a skill issue or some training we need to do to get them where they need to be?

Good management is about getting them to that minimum expectation. Leadership then takes that to the next level, to go beyond the expectation: "Hey, do you understand why this is important? What are some of the barriers you're facing? How can I help you perform better to get you well above 90 percent?" You can see how this combination of management and leadership becomes incredibly effective to not only ensure people are meeting the minimum expectations, but are also motivated to go beyond them.

> **TIP:** I find that poor performance usually comes down to one of three things: lack of motivation, lack of perspiration, or lack of skill. I can help with motivation through great leadership. I can help with skill through great management. I can't help with perspiration. If I've done my best on the motivation and skill side of things, but someone simply isn't willing to put in the effort, that's when I make the decision to make them available to the free market economy.

Meetings: Leadership and Management in Action

Before we move into business systems, I'd like to address an important example of leadership and management in action: meetings. Meetings are a vital part of running any business, yet they're one of the biggest pain points for dentists because we were never taught how to run them in school. I've had so many dentists come to me asking questions about meetings—how to run them, what types of meetings to have, and how frequently to have them.

And it makes sense. Running a meeting can be stressful, and it's even more stressful if you don't have a system to rely on. In order to have efficient, productive, and inspiring meetings, you need to have the right systems in place to run them efficiently as well as the right leadership to make them effective. So let's take a look at how meetings should ideally work.

I typically advocate for five types of meetings:

1. **Quarterly One-on-One Meetings**
2. **Morning Huddles**
3. **Afternoon Huddles**
4. **Monthly Team Meetings**
5. **Performance Reviews**

Each of these meetings will be described in detail below, and I've even included agenda templates for all of them on drbenfriberg.com/bookresources. I highly recommend downloading those and using them as you run these meetings. Or at least checking them out and using them as inspiration to create your own agenda templates. It's worth noting that agendas are one of the best ways to ensure your meetings are successful—they're especially important for one-on-ones, monthly team meetings, and performance reviews.

Quarterly One-on-One Meetings

One-on-one meetings are incredibly important, and something many practice owners neglect. I had one client who came to me and told me someone was leaving her office who'd been with her for fifteen years because they "didn't feel they were being supported." My client was totally caught by surprise—she had no idea this person was feeling that way and was shocked they'd never come to her for support. So I asked her, "When did you provide them the opportunity to do that?" She couldn't say.

If you don't provide the opportunity for your employees to speak openly and candidly with you about their role and what's going on in their lives, you're never going to know. For a long time, I had an open-door policy in my practice. That meant my door was always open for anyone on my team to come and tell me what was going on. I thought this would be a great way for us to stay connected and for me to keep informed on what was happening in the office.

Well, what actually happened was that no one came to me until things were really, really bad. People would come to me saying they used to love working in my practice, but they were thinking about quitting. Or that they were already interviewing at another job because they weren't enjoying working at my practice. Man, that gutted me. I'm so grateful for their bravery to even mention that to me instead of just putting in their two-week's notice or leaving on bad terms. That goes back to psychological safety and my leadership philosophy—they knew it was safe to say those things and that I'd listen.

The lesson was that I needed to be much more intentional about connecting with my team. One-on-one meetings don't have to be some long drawn-out process; they just need to happen on a consistent basis, and they need to be mandatory. I schedule twenty minutes of one-on-one time with each of my employees once per quarter. Every three months, I intentionally sit down and talk with every person, and it's a two-way conversation. You can, of course, decide on a meeting length and cadence that works for you—the important thing is that it's scheduled, and you intentionally dedicate time toward it.

These meetings should be a safe space. They're meant to be a two-way conversation where your employee can tell you everything they need to tell you without fear of judgment or "getting in trouble." Your job in these meetings is simply to listen to what they're saying and learn how you can better support them. Ask questions like, "How can I better support you?" and "How can I help you get what you want out of this position?" Your job as the employer is to find what motivates your employees and then do everything you can to give it to them. This is where you do that, and if done right, you'll be able to create loyalty and longevity among your team.

The bigger your organization, the harder this will be. In some situations, you may need to delegate some one-on-one meetings to other managers. But what's important is that employees come into an open two-way communication system where they can tell you what's going on. And ideally, they get some time to talk to you one-on-one on a routine basis.

Since I've implemented one-on-one meetings, there have been far less challenges to team morale because I have much more visibility on what's happening within the practice. I'm being told things that my team would otherwise keep from me. And once again, this is another form of positive reinforcement—I'm showing them that I take their needs, wants, desires, opinions, and feelings seriously. So next time something happens, they're more likely to bring it up.

There's also something humanizing about this whole experience. We've talked about the chasm of isolation, which goes both ways. There's a lot of separation between any boss and employee, but as a dentist, it's even more so. Your employees are likely to place you on a bit of a pedestal—they view you as their boss, someone who they have to behave perfectly around. They probably don't feel like they can be themselves around you.

These one-on-one meetings are a great chance to simply connect with your employees on a more human level and show them that they *can* be themselves around you. It's an opportunity to develop a unique relationship with each person that goes beyond the workplace. Sometimes, if one of my employees doesn't have much to tell me about their role, we'll just talk about their lives. I'm so thankful for moments like that because we're both able to bond on a deeper level and feel less isolated at work. If you don't intentionally create those opportunities to just sit down and talk, those conversations probably aren't going to happen.

> **TIP:** I have a simple mantra with my team: *You're either upset enough that it matters and you need to address it, or you're not upset enough to bring it up and you have to forgive and let it go completely.* There's no middle ground.
>
> My team knows that if there's a problem, they can't hold on to it. They also know that if it's not a big enough problem to bring to me, they need to let it go. Anything in the middle creates bitterness, which destroys the relationship. This is something we talk about, and I'd suggest talking about it with your team too.

Morning Huddles

Morning huddles are something every practice should incorporate if they haven't already. This is simply a chance to set the tone for the day and ensure everyone is aligned and prepared for whatever is set to unfold that day. In my practice, our morning huddles involve the entire team—the front office staff, dental assistants, hygienists, and myself. We keep these meetings short and focused, typically around fifteen minutes.

We start by going through the day's schedule, discussing each patient and any specific concerns or needs. This might include noting if a patient is particularly anxious, has allergies, or if there were any issues during their last visit. For example, if a patient mentioned being unhappy with their last experience, we make sure everyone is aware so we can go the extra mile to turn things around for them.

We also use this as an opportunity to find ways to optimize our schedule and provide better care. For example, if we notice a patient coming in for a cleaning has outstanding treatment that needs to be done, and we have an open slot in the schedule, we'll discuss the possibility of completing that treatment on the same day.

This is all standard stuff. What might not be so standard, however, is what comes next. Every morning in our huddle, I ask each team member to share something they're grateful for. It could be as simple as "I'm grateful the Starbucks line was short this morning," or "I'm grateful for the time I got to spend with my friends last night." This just helps us get into a positive mindset for the day. One thing you won't hear my team say is, "I'm grateful that I don't have to work tomorrow!" We don't want to celebrate the fact that we don't have to work, because work is supposed to be something we enjoy. (And we do enjoy it!)

Next, each person picks a core value they'll focus on that day. This is probably the number-one strategy for keeping my team aligned with our vision, mission, and core values. This simple action ensures they have our core values memorized, and it means they'll have one specific core value in the back of their mind throughout the day. It's a great way to remind my team of how I expect them to be operating on a daily basis.

We end the morning huddle with a check-in. One of our core values is "be supportive," and this is one way we exemplify that. At the end of every morning huddle, I open up the conversation to allow anyone to share anything that's happening in their lives that may affect their work that day. So someone might say, "Hey guys, I didn't sleep very well. I'm not feeling my best. So if I'm a little slow with you today, that's why." Now we know that person isn't feeling great today, and they might be a bit grumpy. That helps us support them and act accordingly throughout the day, ensuring we're providing a five-star experience for our patients no matter what's happening in our personal lives.

The key to these meetings is consistency and participation. Everyone has to be intentional about setting aside the time, showing up, and participating. It's super important. And it might feel awkward at first, but stick with it. Over time, these meetings will become an essential part of your day.

Afternoon Huddles

While morning huddles set us up for success, afternoon huddles help us finish strong and prepare for the next day. These are shorter than our morning huddles, typically lasting only five to ten minutes, but they help ensure we're all on the same page and give us a chance to reflect on what happened that day. Keep these huddles quick. Adult learning theory states that we don't actually learn by doing, but by reflecting on what we've done. So this huddle, even though it's shorter, is important to make sure that reflection and learning happens.

We typically start by going over anything significant that happened during the day and anything we need for the day after. Then, everyone has a chance to speak up and give an example of how they saw another employee enact one of the core values mentioned in the morning huddle. This is another example of reinforcement through praise (and doing so in public), and it further solidifies the core values in everyone's minds.

If people are drained from the day and just want to get home, let them. This isn't meant to be an exhaustive, comprehensive meeting—it's just an opportunity to check in, reflect, give praise, and make sure everyone's ready for the next day.

Monthly Team Meetings

While the morning and afternoon huddles are focused on what's happening right now in our practice, we also hold monthly team meetings to look at the bigger picture. These meetings are about improvement, skill sets, reviewing/creating/monitoring systems, and addressing concerns that require longer conversations. This isn't the time to say, "Hey, make sure you throw out your expired yogurt," but it is the time to say, "Hey, I don't think this process is working—can we think of any ways to improve it?"

There are really two goals for these meetings: to move our practice forward and to create camaraderie. So every four weeks we shut the practice down, turn our phones off, and sit down for two hours to discuss whatever needs to be discussed. Our normal office hours are 8:00 a.m. to 4:00 p.m., but on these days, we'll work until 2:00 p.m. and then shut the practice down for the last two hours of the day. We'll also schedule some type of fun activity after the meeting just to allow everyone to let loose for a bit and have those meaningful conversations that can only happen outside of work. That's where the camaraderie part comes in.

Now, any time you're meeting for two hours, you need to have some structure so things don't go off the rails. I don't want to waste two hours of my own time, and I don't want to waste my team's time either—so having an agenda for this meeting is particularly important. The week before the meeting, I ask my team to add anything they want to discuss to a whiteboard in our office, which becomes our agenda. And this can be anything from "The distilled water isn't getting delivered," to "The break room is too messy," to "We're receiving too many complaints about ___." I'll also add my own agenda items to that same list, so all of our thoughts are in one place.

The meeting is then structured into three main parts:

1. **Reviewing leftover agenda items from last month:** We'll start by reviewing any tasks or changes that came out of our last meeting. If we've implemented changes, we'll reflect on those—are they working well? Is there any additional work we need to do? Things we need to tweak?
2. **Discussing new ideas or issues from the agenda:** This is where we start going through the agenda items on the whiteboard. This is the bulk of the meeting where we really get into the weeds on the current state of the practice and how we want to move forward.
3. **Improvement and training:** We'll also dedicate some time to improving our skill sets. This might be around the script we use for phone calls, how we manage a certain procedure, how we communicate as a team, etc. This could be based on what has come up in the meeting or something I've noticed and want to teach the team. Either way, there are always things to learn—and now is a great time to focus on that, rather than during a busy workweek.

One important consideration is to have someone writing down action items throughout the meeting. At the end, you can then review the list of action items that have come out of the meeting and create an accountability structure around who's going to do what and by when. Reviewing that accountability structure then becomes the first part of your next monthly team meeting: "Hey, you said you were going to do X, Y, and Z by this date. Did you? Okay, great! How's it going?" or "No? Why? What prevented you? How can we support you on this?"

We'll follow this meeting up with some type of fun activity. We've done things like axe-throwing, escape rooms, and renting out a bar for a few hours and inviting everyone's friends and family to join us, but it doesn't have to be anything extravagant. After one of our last monthly meetings, we played some games in the office with small cash prizes. It was a great time! It's just about doing something fun to break up the monotony and giving the team something to look forward to after working hard together.

> **TIP:** Please make an effort to not schedule unnecessary meetings or make meetings longer than they need to be. We've all been in a meeting that didn't need to happen, and when it happens often, people start to dread coming to them. Use an agenda and be efficient. If you have two hours scheduled for a meeting and you get through the agenda in one hour, then you all get to leave an hour early! (Your team will thank you!)

Performance Reviews

Performance reviews are essentially more formal one-on-one meetings that are focused on an employee's performance. I start these sixty days into an employee's tenure, which is enough time for them to have a good grasp of their role and expectations.

The process actually starts before the meeting, when I have them fill out a self-evaluation against their job description and some of the metrics we're looking for. It's different for every role, so for a dental assistant it may ask questions like, "How well do you seat the patient?" or "How well do you set up for an implant surgery?" These questions are actually built from their job description, so it gives me a good measure of how they feel they're doing within those core competencies. The cultural questions are more like, "How often are you cheerfully engaging with the team?" or "How often do you participate in team activities?" I ask them to rate themselves on a scale of one to four, with four meaning they're performing at the highest level and one meaning they need significant improvement.

Starting with a self-evaluation is key because it allows the team to participate in their own self-leadership. What usually happens is they course-correct themselves without me needing to interfere. They'll see a question and think, "Well, I actually haven't been doing great at this," and mark themselves accordingly. When it comes time to have the meeting, I then evaluate them from my perspective and compare my scores with theirs. This allows me to approach the conversation much differently. I can note areas where they scored themselves low and say, "Hey, I actually think you're doing much better than that," and I can address more critical feedback by saying, "Okay, I see you're at a two here—what can we do to get you to a four?"

There's a bit more nuance to this that I'm not going to include here for the sake of brevity, but this should give you a starting point.

It Starts with Self-Leadership (Always)

As we move into business systems and the management side of running a seven-figure practice, it's worth taking a step back to remember where this all begins: with you. The ability to lead your team effectively, to create those systems, to implement all the stuff we're about to get into—that's all reliant on you and the way you lead *yourself*.

You can't pour from an empty cup. You need a solid (concrete!) foundation from which to lead others. By taking care of yourself first, you'll become equipped to truly care for your team, make the right decisions, and implement things the right way. If you haven't already, now is the time to get yourself ready for what's to come—to reconnect with your passions, fuel your body, and get your physical and mental health in check. Because it's going to make everything else you do easier, more productive, and more profitable.

As much as I love the nitty-gritty operations stuff, the journey to a seven-figure practice is about way more than systems. I hope you've seen that by now and are taking it seriously. You now have the knowledge to lead yourself well. Be concrete. Be intentional. Lead yourself, and you'll be amazed at how effectively you can lead—and manage!—others.

Define, Refine, Implement

Define: Determine the types and number of meetings you need to implement in your practice.

Refine: Create a set of goals for each of your meetings. Schedule all your meetings for the year and inform your team of them.

Implement: Follow this advice from Nike: "Just do it!"

BUSINESS SYSTEMS

It might surprise you to hear me say that I like a McDonald's hamburger from time to time. (What? I'm a human being!) That said, it's not something my family and I eat frequently. Yet over the years, I've noticed a very specific trend when we travel with our kids. Any time we're outside of the US, my kids seem to crave McDonald's. It doesn't matter if we're in Spain, eating the most incredible cured meats, or handmade pizza in Italy—the longer the trip goes on, the more they ask for McDonald's. Eventually, we give in to their demands.

Now, as much as I'd like my kids to eat healthy all the time, I can totally empathize with them on this one. Being in an entirely new place for an extended period of time is hard enough as an adult. For kids, it's even more challenging—they're totally out of their comfort zone, trying new foods, sleeping in a different bed, hearing different languages. It's only natural for them to want something they're familiar with. It's incredibly comforting for them to be able to walk into a McDonald's and get the same Happy Meal they know and love, regardless of whether they're in Switzerland or Chicago.

You've got to give it to McDonald's—they might not make the highest-quality food, but darn it if they're not consistent. That level of consistency exists because of the incredible business systems they've put in place. And there's a lesson to be learned from this even if you're not planning to launch a gigantic fast-food corporation that spans the globe.

Businesses of all types thrive on consistency. Major corporations like McDonald's, Coca-Cola, and Starbucks know this, and they work extremely hard to ensure near-perfect consistency across their thousands of locations. As healthcare entrepreneurs, our world is a little different, but the same principle applies. The first patient that walks in your door at 8:00 a.m. should be getting the same experience as the last one who walks in at 4:00 p.m. The patient you've known for four years should be getting the same experience as the patient that just sat down in your chair for the first time. The vendor you pay monthly should be getting paid at the same time in February as they did in January. Consistency will make or break any business, and yours is no different.

Systems are the key to consistency. Everything in your business that you want to be predictable, repeatable, consistent, and efficient needs to have a system; a documented process for how it gets done in *your* business, so it's done the same way and produces the same outcome every time, regardless of who's doing it. If you don't have systems in place, you're simply hoping everything works out—and that's not acceptable for any business, let alone one where you're in control of people's health.

When you're thinking about setting up systems in your business, there's really one primary goal: to make the dentist replaceable. You're the dentist and owner, but those are two separate roles. As the owner, your job is to create systems so that the dentist could be replaced tomorrow. And that dentist would be able to come in and do the exact same procedures in the exact same way with the exact same results. Your team would also be able to continue running your business in the exact same way they have been, with the exact same results.

In this chapter, I want you to shift your mindset from "dentist" to "owner." You're the owner of a healthcare business! Act accordingly.

Why Doctors Need Systems

As doctors, I think we all understand the value of a checklist. In Atul Gawande's famous book *The Checklist Manifesto*, he describes how simple checklists reduced deaths in operating rooms by up to 47 percent (along with a whole host of other benefits). When most people hear that fact, they're shocked to learn there was a time when surgeons would even operate on someone without following a specific procedure. For me, it's not that shocking. Why? Because doctors have big egos—and that includes you (and me!).

Seriously—we've been through so much schooling, spent so many years in training, and have so much knowledge that we think we can do everything. Personally, I know I could walk into a crown prep on any tooth and do it 99 percent perfectly without a checklist because I've done it thousands of times. So the idea of a surgeon doing an operation based on their memory, knowledge, and skill alone—it's really not that far-fetched. But given our education, we also know that's not a good idea.

My hunch is that there are many things in your business right now that you do from memory alone. You might not see the need to document them because they're simple. You might think, "I could do this blindfolded. I do it perfectly every time. I'm not going to waste my time writing this down." You're wrong. That's your ego talking. I guarantee that system is more complicated than you think, you're making mistakes you don't realize, and your results are not as consistent as you think they are. Because without a system in place, that's what happens.

The unfortunate reality is that humans are inconsistent. We get complacent. We skip steps because they feel unnecessary. We think our memory is perfect when it's not. As business owners, we're the last line of accountability. Yet historically, the tendency is to be more lenient toward oneself than others. Systems are the only way to remove that inconsistency.

And really, it goes far beyond consistency. Systems are essentially the tools your team needs to do their jobs. Without systems, morale drops, efficiency decreases, and mistakes get made. In one study on the impacts of self-serving leadership (a.k.a. when leaders prioritize their own interests over others), researchers found that self-serving leaders consistently diminished psychological safety, heightened workplace anxiety, and suppressed innovative behaviors across their teams.[ix] No wonder!

Imagine walking into work every day not knowing what you're supposed to do or how to do it. Or constantly worrying that you're doing things wrong. That's a great way to make your employees feel psychologically unsafe, versus walking into a job where you know exactly what you're supposed to do, and you have a step-by-step process you can follow to complete it correctly.

Even things that seem obvious can benefit from being clarified and documented. For example, who is responsible for what? "Everyone" in my practice is responsible for sterilization because it's such an important task. The idea is that we all chip in to make sure it gets done. But still, at the end of the day, the ultimate responsibility falls upon my lead dental assistant. If there's a problem with sterilization, I go to them. And they know that it's their responsibility to ensure it gets done every day—whether that means them doing it personally or reminding the team that they need to stay on top of it.

When things need to get done among groups of people, you have to be specific. There's a psychological phenomenon called the diffusion of responsibility, or "bystander effect," that confirms this. Spoiler alert: You already know this one! Remember your CPR training? If you're conducting CPR on someone, and there's a crowd of people around you, you don't just say, "Someone call 911!"—you point at one person and say, "*You!* Call 911!" That's because diffusion of responsibility states that a person is less likely to take responsibility for action or inaction when other bystanders or witnesses are present.[x] In other words, everyone thinks someone else is going to do it, so no one actually does it.

If it's unclear who's responsible for completing a certain task in your business, there's a good chance it's not going to get done. And not only is it not going to get done, but as a leader, it's now difficult to hold any one person accountable for this mistake. Really, *you* should be held accountable for not clarifying who was supposed to do it in the first place.

There are so many benefits to having the right systems in place within your business. Systems help people understand the rules of the game—they're like bumpers in a bowling alley. When your team has the right systems to support them, they're set up for success. They keep morale high and make your practice an enjoyable place to work. They minimize mistakes and help your team work more efficiently, which leads to higher profitability, better working hours, and less stress.

From a business standpoint, they're essential. They safeguard your business in the event that someone leaves abruptly, since a new employee can come in and learn their role quickly by following your systems. Even if someone calls in sick, with the right systems in place, you can have other team members take over their responsibilities for the day to keep things running—even if they aren't specifically trained in that role (assuming they are legally allowed to do it, of course).

For the owner, systems allow you to remove yourself from daily minutiae. They allow you to delegate more of your workload and free up your time to focus on more important things. If you want to grow your business, you need to have systems in place. This isn't just a suggestion—it's a requirement.

Administrative Days

Entrepreneurs often talk about the difference between working "on" your business versus working "in" your business. When you're building a business, it's not uncommon to find yourself working long hours just to keep things afloat. I refer to this as the "survival stage" of a business. When you're in that mode, the idea of spending additional time on the more administrative stuff like documenting systems or reviewing financial metrics isn't exactly top of mind.

Dentists are no different, and we may even be at the high end of that spectrum. Most dentists are spending the vast majority of their time doing dentistry, as they should. That's great since it makes you money, but it's not great because you'll eventually work yourself to death. It's important to dedicate a certain amount of time to working "on" your business—creating systems that will grow the business and free up your time. This is another one of those situations where intentionally investing time up front will pay dividends in the long run.

I remember when I first started working with a client (and now dear friend) of mine, Yulia, who'd just started her dental practice. She was working full days as a dentist, then at night she would shift to "owner" and spend long hours working on the business side of her practice—which is all too common in our industry. She had what seemed like a million things to do, all of which felt terribly urgent in the moment. I could see that she was not only setting herself on a path toward burnout, but that many of these seemingly "urgent" tasks weren't actually going to make or break her business.

I gave her two simple pieces of advice, which I'll give to you as well: *Stop working at night, and focus on one thing at a time.* I know it might seem like you need to drop everything and get your business running like a well-oiled machine overnight, but that's not going to happen—and it probably doesn't need to happen right away.

My recommendation is to schedule at least one day per month as an "administrative day" where you don't do dentistry and you work exclusively "on" your business. If you can do this bi-weekly, even better. This is your time to come into the office *alone* and put on your entrepreneur hat. My brother Josh is a real estate coach, but he coaches business owners in other industries as well. He and I often talk about how valuable administrative days are for all entrepreneurs, and we've even gone so far as to suggest buying a hat that says "Entrepreneur." When you have your loops on, you're working *in* your business as the dentist. But when you take those loops off and put that physical hat on, you're a healthcare entrepreneur—and now you're working *on* the business.

I'm going to be asking a lot of you in the following chapters. Don't feel like you need to set this all up overnight. As you go through, take notes on what's coming up for you and where you might want to focus your efforts. Figure out the order of priority for those tasks, schedule your admin days, and then forget about it until that day comes. When it does, you'll know exactly what you need to focus on. And stop working at night!

Mindset for System Creation

Assuming I've successfully convinced you of the need for systems in your business, let's move on to the "how." Systems creation starts with the right mindset. Any time you want to document, implement, or change something in your business, it needs a system—and the system needs to be made in advance. The same goes for things in your business that you're currently doing without one. Those activities need to be revisited and given a proper system.

There's a process you can use for this—dare I say it, a *system for implementing systems.* (Thrilling, I know.) Luckily for you, you already know this. It's *define, refine, implement.* The process of creating a new system or revising an old one falls perfectly into the DRI framework:

Step 1: *Define* the goal of the system you want to document, implement, or change.

Step 2: *Refine* and document the process for how you'll fulfill that system.

Step 3: *Implement* the refined system, monitor the results, and adjust accordingly.

Really, it's just common sense—but the reality is that many owners don't follow those steps. Or they even do them in the exact opposite order. Entrepreneurs often get excited about new ideas, especially new opportunities to generate revenue. Sometimes, we have more optimism than sense. We get so caught up in the potential of this new thing that we get started without thinking through everything we need to do to implement it successfully. Then we don't get the results we were expecting, so we either drop it—in which case the whole thing ends up being a waste of time—or spend an exorbitant amount of time, effort, and money fixing problems we could've avoided in the first place.

I'll admit I've been that person. Four years ago, I started offering clear aligner therapy in the form of Invisalign, and I didn't define or refine this process before implementing it. I just bought the scanner and announced, "We're doing Invisalign now!" That's it. As you can imagine, it didn't go well.

That was a proverbial grenade toss to my team. They know Invisalign exists, they know that it works sometimes, and that's about it. When I made that announcement, I was hit with a barrage of questions, uncertainty, frustration, and disillusionment from my team. I basically made every mistake you could in terms of leadership and management. Not to mention all the financial and logistical problems I created. I hadn't thought about how to market this, so it was difficult to acquire patients. I hadn't trained my team on everything they needed to do, so the first treatments were disastrous. I could go on. It took years to iron out all the wrinkles I had inadvertently made by not planning ahead. Perhaps this sounds familiar?

Now, when I take a continuing education course that will involve a change in clinical practice, I use the DRI framework. And part of that, as you'll see, involves preempting my team and even involving them in the decisions around how to implement it.

It's important to let your team know that changes are coming in advance. For instance, we have started to implement full-mouth rehab dentistry in our practice. At one of our monthly team meetings, I let my team know about the courses I'd be taking and what type of dentistry we'd be incorporating, and encouraged everyone to start thinking of questions, problems, and solutions we might be faced with. They were going to be involved in fulfilling those procedures, and they know more about their roles than I do, so I wanted to make sure they had an equal stake in how this thing got done. We had some proper brainstorming and the end result was far better—and easier!—than if I'd just sat down on my own and written a process for them to follow.

If you just tell them about some "new thing" and immediately ask for feedback, you'll end up with blank stares and uneasy team members. Give them time to process, and be sure to include them—it affects them too!

Now, you can probably already envision how DRI would apply to systems creation. But let's break it down and look at a few real-world examples so you can see how this actually works.

Define

Any time you're thinking about documenting, implementing, or changing something in your business, you need to clearly define the goal you're trying to accomplish. This ensures that when you go to build the system, you're building it in a way that will accomplish that goal.

The define step is about stopping yourself and saying, "I want x. And I want this system to do y." I know, it sounds unnecessary—but once again, this is about being intentional. Just like your vision guides your practice, this statement guides the creation of your system. If your goal is for this change to increase revenue, then you'll be reminded of that during the system creation and look for ways to ensure it increases revenue. Without stating that, you're more likely to ignore opportunities to increase revenue or lower cost in favor of getting the thing done. And when you share this defining statement with your team, then they also know to speak up if they notice areas where revenue might be impacted.

If you're revisiting an old system, this step is still valuable to ensure what you've been doing is aligned with the goal you're trying to accomplish. That will then dictate how you change or create the system.

This step could take thirty seconds or it could take thirty minutes. Sometimes it will be obvious, but sometimes, when you dig deeper, you'll realize this thing is a little more nuanced than you might have realized. Sometimes, you might even realize this system you're thinking of isn't actually going to accomplish your goal and, therefore, isn't worth implementing. In that case, you've just saved yourself a whole bunch of time, money, and headache.

And by the way, I'm not immune from this either. Take, for example, my obsession with 3D printers! 3D printers are an amazing technology that can be used in nearly every step of dental treatment. I've sold myself on buying a 3D printing system on more than one occasion, and I think my dental supply rep is getting tired of sending me quotes. Why haven't I bought one yet? Because if I were to incorporate 3D printing into our practice at this point in time, it would either break our systems or go underutilized.

The reason is because we have a very efficient schedule for our desired workflow. Our assistants are busy all day, every day. I'm busy all day, every day. All of which is great. But that means that to add this technology, we would first need to do the following:

1. Find space to put the printer, which would involve a significant rearranging of limited space.
2. Train everyone (including me!) on how to use and troubleshoot the new 3D printing hardware, software, and materials.
3. Figure out who's going to do what by when and all of the other critical tasks required to implement this new system.

We simply don't have the capacity to take that on right now. If we did take it on, the only way it could work is if some other critical tasks took a back seat—or if we just bought it and didn't use it. Either way, it's not a great situation. Could this change in the future?

Absolutely. That's why we regularly reevaluate if "now is the right time" to buy that 3D printer.

One important factor to consider here is that adding a system doesn't create linear complexity, it creates *exponential complexity*. Those three items I listed? When you dig into the details, there's really more like six actual things that need to get done—and that's just the tip of the iceberg. Not only that, but you're talking about clarifying all that across a team. The more you add into your business, the more exponentially complicated it gets. Because you're not just adding "one" new thing—you're adding the thing, building a system for it, training multiple people, changing multiple people's workflows, dealing with new problems that arise. The list goes on.

My business systems professor would be proud. I've finally learned to "keep it simple, stupid." I suggest you do the same.

Refine

Once you've defined the change and clarified what you want the system to accomplish, you need to refine it by creating the system. This is by far the most time-intensive part of the process, and for good reason. What you do here will dictate how successful this change will be.

Refining the process involves clarifying exactly how it will get done and how all the various stakeholders will be impacted. For that reason, it's absolutely vital that you include your team in this part of the process. I typically use our monthly team meetings for this. I'll define the change on my own, give my team advanced notice that we're going to be talking about this in the next monthly meeting, and then use that time to start refining the system.

In that meeting, we critically analyze the impact to as many key stakeholders as we can. We'll even assign key stakeholders to team members. Following, I've included a list of the typical stakeholders we consider any time we look at implementing a new system. Note that these questions can easily be reframed for documenting or changing a current system.

1. **The Patient:** Who is the patient we are targeting? What are their primary goals in seeking out this kind of treatment? What are their barriers to care?
2. **The Doctor:** Does the doctor want to do this procedure? Where, when, and how will the continuing education take place? How much will it cost to adequately learn and skillfully provide this service? When will the procedure be performed?
3. **The Dental Assistant:** Do they have adequate training and resources to fulfill this? Are they comfortable providing this procedure? Are there any skill or confidence gaps in communication?
4. **The Hygienist:** How will this impact their position? What role will they play in patient education? Will it require more time to provide high-level care during appointments?
5. **Office Administrator:** How will this be billed? When and how will it be paid for? What codes will be used? What will the fee structure be? What documents should be created? What consent forms need to be added? How does this impact scheduling? How will we inform existing and new patients about this procedure?
6. **Infrastructure:** Does the office need to purchase new equipment? Inventory? Storage? Are there technology considerations like servers or computers? Are there sterilization requirements?
7. **Interested Third Parties:**
    a. **Payers:** Will third-party payers pay for this service? Do they offer enough coverage? Do we need to look for a new provider?
    a. **Liability Insurance:** Is this service currently covered? Does the practice have enough coverage for the new equipment? Will there need to be a new policy created?
    a. **Licensing Board:** Do we have everything required to satisfy the board? Are there specific requirements in

reporting and recording?
8. **Vendors and Suppliers:** Is everything in place to order what we need? Are there limitations we face with specific vendors or suppliers? Do we have alternatives if something is backordered or out of stock? How will our marketing company adjust our website and advertising budget to adequately supply new patients?
9. **"What Else?":** This is one of the most powerful questions to keep asking until it hurts a little. How will this impact our reputation? Is this a fad? Does it align with our vision, mission, and core values?
10. **Profitability:** How will this impact our profit? Costs versus fee? Have we considered the opportunity cost? (What aren't we able to do because we're doing this?)

These are the nitty-gritty questions you need to be asking yourself and your team if you want your system to be successful. You can see how, if you were to work through these questions carefully, you could avoid a lot of potential problems before they occur—or be prepared when they do. And because you've thought about how this will impact all key stakeholders, everyone will be prepared when that new system arrives, and they'll know exactly what they need to do to make it work.

As you refine your system, you should be documenting everything. The goal is that by the end of this step, you and your team are clear on everything that needs to happen to successfully implement the system, and there's a step-by-step process for how to fulfill it. That step-by-step process should be created by the person (or people) who will be working within the system. This is extremely important because that person likely knows more than you do about what needs to happen to fulfill this. It all comes back to leadership. Letting them dictate how things get done within their role is motivating. It's an opportunity for them to make a difference. When they have ownership over the process, they're more likely to do it. They're also more likely to offer up ways to improve it or point out areas that aren't working. If you just create the system yourself and tell your team this is how you want it done, that's managing—not leading. And you're not nearly as likely to get the kind of feedback you need to improve the system.

By the way, sometimes you might start refining only to realize the system isn't worth it. Maybe it's not actually going to produce the results you want. Or maybe the needs of your business have shifted since you started, and it's no longer relevant. Or maybe you realize this thing you've always done that you wanted to "optimize" was never actually worth doing in the first place. That's great! Ditch it. You've just avoided wasting your time, money, and effort on something that isn't going to move the needle.

I once worked with a dentist who went to a seminar for this new type of facial rejuvenation procedure, and when I spoke with her afterward, she was all excited about adding it to her business. The equipment was around $150,000, but she could theoretically make that money back in around six months based on what the company was telling her she could charge and how many procedures she could do per day. I could practically see the dollar signs in her eyes. Just buy the thing and start selling it! It will all work out. Right?

Having been there myself, I could understand her excitement. This *could* potentially be a great addition to her business, but it was also a very complicated system to implement. There was a lot to think through. So I started asking her questions.

- Do you want to do this?
- Will you enjoy doing this?
- Do you have the capacity to do it?
- Most people come to you for dental work, not facial rejuvenation, so do you have the clientele to support this?
- This would be an entirely new sales process—are you prepared for that?
- What is your clients' expectation of cost versus what the facial rejuvenation company says you can charge?

- How will this impact your dentistry?
- Would you be better off using that time and effort to perform more dentistry?

As we started working through those initial questions, there was a lot of hesitation. She realized that it was going to be very difficult to implement and find new patients for this type of procedure. Ultimately, she ended up not implementing it in her business for that reason.

If you get through this *refine* process and you're still excited about it, your team is excited about it, and it's clear that this new thing will be a net positive for your business—absolutely implement it. But if you're feeling hesitant, listen to that instinct. It's either a sign you need to think this through more carefully or the system may not be worth implementing.

Implement

Now, and only now, are you ready to implement. If you've followed the steps up to this point, it should go smoothly. Simply follow the system you've developed and monitor the initial outcome. Ask yourself these questions:

- Does it work?
- Are we getting the results we expected?
- Is this a net positive?
- Does the team have any feedback?
- Can we improve this?

Your work doesn't end after implementation. You can't just hope this system has solved your problem or that you're better off than you were. Be prepared to monitor your progress and adjust the system as needed. We've taken many steps to ensure you're successful, but chances are, you're not going to get it perfect the first time.

Maybe there's a redundant step in the process, or you've assigned someone to a specific task that's put them over capacity, and they're now feeling overworked. Talk with your team and watch closely.

If it's not a net positive, circle back and go through a new *refine* process to analyze the system and figure out how to get things working. (The good news for you is that this second pass isn't nearly as in-depth—usually it's just a couple of tweaks.) I treat this part like I would treat performance reviews with a new employee, albeit a little less structured. I typically follow up with my team within the first week to see how the system is working from their perspective: "How's the new system going?" "Do we feel like it's flowing well?" "Have you encountered any problems?"

I'll follow up a week later, then again in a month, and then again in ninety days. It can take some time for issues to arise, and as your team gets more familiar with the system, they may find opportunities to improve it. It's important to circle back and address those issues to make sure everything is running smoothly. And I hate to say it, but this process never really "ends."

Business Systems Are "Living Documents"

Ideally, I would love to create a business system, perfect it, and then never touch it again—just ship it off to my team and sit back while they perform everything perfectly for the next decade. Unfortunately, that's just not possible, even though many business owners seem to think it is. Every system in your business is a living document, and you should be in the habit of routinely revisiting, updating, and optimizing them. Think of this as maintenance for your business, just like you'd do routine oil changes on your car or floss your teeth. (Because all dentists floss daily. *Right?*)

In our practice, we spend part of our monthly meeting on this. I open it up to the team: "What challenges are we having with our systems?" "What's been coming up?" "Why do you think that's happening?" "How can we fix it?" We'll often realize that one or a few of our systems aren't working as intended. In rare cases, you may even realize that an entire system needs to be scrapped or reworked. As I write this, there's one situation from my business that immediately comes to mind. As you read, see if you can spot the mistakes we made. I'll reveal them at the end.

Years ago, long before I created the DRI framework and shared it with my team, we had an intern create a system for following up with referrals. When we referred a patient to a specialist, we wanted to verify that they were contacted and ultimately seen by the specialist. This is just an extra step we wanted to take to ensure continuity of care. I don't want one of my patients' oral health to be affected by someone forgetting to make a phone call.

So this intern created an entire system to make sure we were following up with our referral offices. They made a nice book with cells and boxes, and the idea was that when we referred someone, we'd write down the patient's name and the office(s) we'd referred them to in this book. Then, every week, the administrative team would go through the book and call those referral offices to make sure they received the referral, called the patient, and booked an appointment. We'd even track the outcome of the appointment to ensure they received the care they needed.

It was great! The book looked amazing and this system accomplished everything we wanted it to—in theory. Months went by, and frankly, I forgot about it. I finally checked in with my team, and they'd forgotten about it too. The book was practically empty, and we hadn't followed up with our referrals for well over a month. The system wasn't working.

So, what mistakes did we make? The most glaring mistake was that we had an intern create the system instead of the person who would actually be doing the follow-ups. The intern did a great job creating the system, but they created it in a way that worked for them—not the person doing it. The book was cumbersome and not organized effectively for the person doing the follow-ups.

The intern also essentially created this in a vacuum. They didn't get feedback from our team or the referral offices we'd be contacting.

We obviously should have incorporated the team's feedback, but we also should have asked those offices about the most efficient way to exchange this information from their end. Maybe there was a way we could set up some type of automated system to keep track of this? Maybe they already had a system in place that they used with other dentists? We'd never know unless we asked.

And the mistakes didn't stop there! We hadn't clarified which specific person would be responsible for this task, so everyone thought someone else was going to do it, meaning it never got done. I also failed to follow up with my team to see how the system was working. And finally, we failed by not bringing it up in our monthly team meetings.

This is a perfect example of how *not* to implement a new system. And as the leader, I take full responsibility for that. That intern actually did a fantastic job in creating that book—but I failed them by not setting them up for success. That's on me.

A Systems Case Study

When we talk about implementing systems in your dental practice, it's important to prioritize the most critical areas of your business first. One such critical area is training new team members. Let's take a deep dive into how we approach this at Thrive Family Dental so you can see how this works in practice.

We have an extremely comprehensive, step-by-step training system that every new assistant goes through. This system is intentionally structured to start with the most critical elements of the job and work down to the more procedural aspects. Here's how it works:

Day one focuses entirely on documentation and compliance. New assistants come in on a non-patient day so we can dedicate our full attention to covering HIPAA, OSHA, and all state-specific legal requirements. This ensures we're fully compliant from day one. We *have* to do this before we can move on to anything else.

Next, we cover emergency protocols. There are a handful of

protocols we have that detail exactly what to do in an emergency situation, and we prioritize teaching new assistants these protocols first because there could literally be lives on the line. For example, we have a specific code word in our practice for medical emergencies. My team typically refers to me as Dr. Friberg, and if they ever address me as Ben, that's our code for a medical emergency. If someone says, "Ben, you're needed in OPT2," I know immediately there's a medical emergency in that operatory, and that whether I'm in the middle of a crown prep or on an important phone call, I have to drop everything and respond.

This type of systematic communication prevents panic and maintains patient confidentiality. We don't want to announce, "Medical emergency in room two!" and freak out every patient in the practice. This system also includes clear protocols for what happens next: one team member calls 911, another meets emergency responders outside, and, if needed, someone helps escort other patients to the waiting room. Everyone on my team knows these protocols inside and out. There's not only a system for the protocols themselves, but a system to teach this during our training process.

After emergency protocols, we move on to sterilization—another critical area where there needs to be a clear system. Assistants learn exactly how instruments should be cleaned, sterilized, and organized to ensure safe patient care. Only after mastering these foundational elements do we move into the actual procedural parts of their job—how to set up trays, prepare rooms, and ultimately assist chairside. And then the final phase covers day-to-day operational systems like clinical notes and end-of-day procedures.

By this point, the assistant has a clear understanding of our vision, mission, core values, safety protocols, and treatment systems—from the most critical aspects of the job down to the specific way we prefer instruments to be handed over during procedures. This systematic approach to training ensures nothing critical is missed and that team members understand not just what to do, but why we do it that way. It's a perfect example of how having well-documented systems can create consistency and efficiency while also potentially saving lives. (It's also kind of a meta example, since it's essentially a system that teaches people how to operate within our systems, which I find very satisfying.)

Now, it's important to consider that we've achieved this level of detail and effectiveness by repeatedly applying our *define*, *refine*, *implement* framework to this process. Our training system wasn't created overnight—it has been continuously refined over many iterations based on what works, what doesn't, and feedback from our team. We've prioritized getting this particular system right because it's so fundamental to our practice's success. When you're running a dental practice, there are countless systems you could focus on improving. The key is to identify which ones are most critical to your business and start there. For us, ensuring new team members are properly trained in a systematic way that emphasizes safety and quality care has been one of our highest priorities.

Systems: An Applied Science

If there's one thing I'd like you to take away from this chapter, it would simply be the importance of adopting a systems-driven mindset. If you're thinking, "Oh my god, I have to go into my practice tomorrow and review every system we have and update all of them and train my team on DRI and . . . !" First, calm down. And second, that's not really what I'm asking of you.

Now, get ready, because I'm going to say it again: *You have to be intentional.* I wouldn't recommend scrapping everything and redoing all your systems tomorrow, or even this week. Take a gradual approach. *Adopt the systems-driven mindset.* As you work in your business, intentionally think of ways to systemize your work or your team's work. When you have that mindset and you start intentionally looking for better ways of operating, things will gradually improve. When you notice something that feels a bit off, make a note to revisit it with your team at the next monthly team meeting. When you're presented with some new idea that could add a revenue stream for your business, think it through in terms of DRI—and maybe revisit this chapter to remind yourself of the more specific instructions. Start by focusing on the areas that are most broken or most consequential if things go wrong, then work your way down from there.

And while I feel confident in the "system for creating systems" framework I've outlined here, I'd also encourage you to think about how *you* want to develop systems that will work best in your practice and with your team. *It's your practice.* That means you can set up your systems in whatever way works best for you. Just remember the overall goals we discussed at the beginning. When you're adding systems to your business, you should be striving to make the dentist replaceable. That doesn't mean you'll be out of a job—it just means you'll have more time, less stress, and an efficient business. In other words, you'll be well on your way to a fulfilling, profitable seven-figure practice.

Define, Refine, Implement

Define: List all the systems you have in your business that you think are inadequately documented.

Refine: Prioritize the systems that have the biggest impact on your business and then schedule time with your team to make a strategic plan around when you're going to update these systems (in order of importance).

Implement: Create and implement the systems!

METRICS AND KPIS

For the last few years, I've gotten into training and competing in endurance sports. I enjoy the discipline—the physical, mental, and even spiritual benefits from consistent training and exertion. Much of this book has been written in my head while running or biking for hours at a time. (Not so much swimming, as I'm focused solely on not drowning.) With endurance sports comes a litany of gadgets and devices to help with training. My watch records over thirty different metrics when I swim. My bike computer will record close to fifty metrics. During my run, my watch will record over forty different metrics. There are normal metrics that most people are familiar with like speed, distance, cadence, and heart rate; and then there are metrics that get *deep* into the data.

For example, my watch gives me a dataset for my average vertical oscillation ratio. I have no idea what that's for, what it means, or what I'm supposed to do with it. One of the metrics on my bike computer is torque effectiveness—another measurement that's meaningless to me. To get any value from these metrics, I'd need to record, read, interpret, and make some sort of meaningful change to my training program to improve the metric.

A metric is meaningless without the subsequent steps of reading it, interpreting it, creating a plan to improve it, and then implementing change to see that improvement come to life. One metric for my run—something I struggle with consistently—is ground contact time. I had no idea what this was or why it mattered until I started having significant knee pain that was preventing me from hitting my goals. I met with my running coach and physical therapist and found I was in pain because my strides were too slow, too long, and I was hitting the ground too hard. I was then given a list of drills and exercises to improve my speed, strength, and form to reduce my ground contact time, which would improve my running efficiency and reduce the load on my knees. I can now run further than I ever have before, and without knee pain.

A business metric is similar to these physical performance metrics in many ways. Just like my watch can give me every metric under the sun, there's a seemingly endless list of business metrics. But without proper knowledge, interpretation, and meaningful change, they're worthless. Yes, you read that correctly—they are *worthless*. (Keep in mind that you don't necessarily need the knowledge or skills to interpret these metrics yourself since you can always rely on the wisdom of outside experts. The point is that if you don't interpret these metrics and use them to create positive change, they're just meaningless numbers.)

One dental metric that gets a lot of attention is called case acceptance rate, which is the percentage of patients who move forward and schedule treatment as recommended by the dentist. Some experts will say you want this number as high as possible, while others offer a range of percentages a healthy practice should fall within. Just looking at the metric alone and coming to a conclusion that you're within the healthy range is often ineffective at truly getting everything out of your practice. Without analysis of the bigger picture, a metric alone can lead to missed opportunity. What if your case acceptance rate is in the top 5 percent of dentists in the nation? Pat yourself on the back—unless your case value size and revenue per patient is in the bottom 5 percent. Metrics are not stand-alone numbers. Without thoughtful and comprehensive interpretation, they can lead practices into a false sense of security that everything is okay when it's not.

This is often illustrated by setting production goals and nothing else. I've worked with several doctors who rely entirely on two KPIs—production and bank account balance. They manage their entire business by trying to increase production and then set their budgets on the whimsical nature of their bank account and an arbitrary number for their balance that will make them feel "comfortable." When a team member asks, "Hey, can we buy a new Cavitron?" the answer is, "Sure! We just need to make sure we produce more next month." Then, a few months later, the team is being told, "Production is down this month, so make sure we only buy what's absolutely necessary for supplies!" I've heard my clients say these things, and while it might be okay in certain situations, there's a better, more predictable way to run a practice.

KPIs: Analysis and Meaningful Change

So, what does it really mean to analyze a metric? Well, it often comes down to simply thinking logically through how a metric works and all the variables in your practice that affect it. The more you learn about metrics, the more comfortable you'll get taking on new ones and figuring out how to interpret them. One of the simplest ways to analyze a metric is to track your numbers, notice their trends, and compare them to industry standards. This is an easy way to make your metrics "mean something." If you're performing at or above industry standards, great! If you're below industry standards, that's a sign you need to make some changes.

Reviewing trends over time is also helpful. If your collections dip every September, you can then get to the bottom of why that change is occurring and what needs to happen to prevent it. (Yes,

"Sucktember" is a very real thing, and I've actually included an example of how I handled this situation later on.) Or if another metric is slowly decreasing over time, you can start experimenting with certain changes to see how they affect the metric. Situations like these might feel troubling at first—"Oh no! We're doing something wrong!"—but really, they're opportunities to improve. Analyzing a metric could open your eyes to problems in your business that are easily fixed and will help you generate more revenue, save money, save time, improve the patient experience, or lead to any number of improvements. These are things you likely wouldn't have found otherwise.

I encountered a situation like this in my own practice with case acceptance rate. I track our case acceptance rate on a weekly basis, and it's calculated by the number of patients that have scheduled treatment versus the amount of treatment plans presented. (If I present a treatment plan for four quadrants of fillings and they schedule one quadrant, that counts as an accepted case.) My goal is to be at 90 percent or higher. When I see a drop in this KPI, it's a signal that there's something to improve on. During our huddles, I'll confer with my team about how we're doing on building rapport, offering our comfort menu, building trust through personalized goal-setting with our patients, and offering flexible payment options.

These are all things that reduce the barriers to "yes," meaning they increase our case acceptance rate KPI. This practice of continual monitoring and adjusting allows us to maximize our time and efficiency. This is also an important KPI to track closely because it has a dramatic impact on other KPIs that we'll cover soon like collections, average patient value, chair time utilization, and profit.

Later in the chapter, I'm going to do a deep dive on specific metrics with lots of nitty-gritty details—which I hope you'll find as thrilling as I do. In the meantime, though, I've developed a simple questionnaire to help you gauge where you currently are with respect to metrics. If you're totally new to KPIs and metrics, you might not have much to fill out—in which case the rest of this chapter will be very useful to you. If none of this is "new" to you, I'd still recommend reading through to ensure you're thinking about these metrics correctly.

Remember that these KPIs alone don't mean much on their own, but analyzing them will help you fine-tune your practice. Once you start regularly measuring these KPIs, you can start improving them. And if your numbers are already looking good, you can use them to start praising your amazing team. KPIs are powerful tools.

Some of these KPIs I track on a daily basis, like patient acquisition rate. Others I track quarterly, like fee-for-service/insurance (FFS/PPO) percentage or revenue percentage based on service type. The key is to have your finger on the pulse of your practice. So take a minute, open your reports from your practice management software and CPA, and see how many KPIs you can record.

If you're struggling to find these numbers, don't know what they mean, or want help interpreting them, the rest of this chapter will be a helpful start—but this is an indicator that it might also be a good time to find a business coach to help you level up your entrepreneurial knowledge. (You can find out more about business coaching atdrbenfriberg.com/bookresources.)

KPI QUESTIONNAIRE

Practice Metrics:

1. What's your current active patient count?
2. What's your new patient acquisition rate?
3. What's your average production per patient?
4. What's your patient retention rate?
5. What percentage of your patients are fee-for-service versus insurance?

Collections and Revenue:
1. What's your collection rate?
2. What's your accounts receivable aging breakdown?
3. What's your insurance claims rejection rate?
4. How long does it typically take to collect outstanding payments?

Operational Efficiency:
1. What's your chair utilization rate?
2. What's your cancellation/no-show rate?
3. What's your overhead percentage relative to revenue?
4. How do you track and manage dental supplies inventory?

Growth and Profitability:
1. What's your year-over-year revenue growth rate?
2. What's your EBITDA margin?
3. What percentage of revenue comes from different service categories?
4. What marketing investments generate the best ROI?

Metrics Deep Dive

During my time in the construction industry, I learned quickly how important it was to have an in-depth understanding of what was going on in every project. Much like dentistry, there were production and income reports—but if that's all the information you relied on, it would be impossible to improve profit. We recorded daily billable production, labor hour efficiency, budget overrun, foreman performance benchmarks, client retention and satisfaction. The list goes on. I loved (and still do) an Excel spreadsheet.

I brought this same data-driven mindset to dentistry, and when I got serious about starting my own practice, I went *deep* on dental metrics and KPIs. I researched endlessly, read books, and spent countless hours figuring out ways to track them, interpret them, and build goals based on them. Looking back, this knowledge has been instrumental in building my practice to what it is today. And as much as I love a good spreadsheet, I'm also happy that we now have dashboards from companies like ADIT or Dental Intelligence to provide this information in a more digestible format.

That being said, I understand that this isn't everyone's cup of tea. That's fine. That's also why, from the moment I realized I wanted to write a book, I knew I wanted to include a deep dive on the most important metrics you need to understand to be a successful practice owner. Now, to be fair, I could've gone much deeper than this—but I think my editor would've killed me. For each metric, I've done my best to provide a succinct description, the recommended value, and suggestions on how to improve it.

The metrics we'll be looking at:

- Gross Production
- Net Production
- Collections
- Collections per Hour
- Overhead and Its Sub-Metrics: Wages, Dental Supplies, Labs
- Profit Margin
- Active Patients
- New Patients Scheduled and Seen
- Average Production per Patient (Annual Patient Value)
- Case Acceptance Rates
- Cancellation or No-Show Rate
- Hygiene Chair Utilization

If you're struggling to make it through this section, that's fine. You're welcome to skip this for now, but I'd urge you to revisit it later. Learning to track and analyze these metrics will be one of the most valuable and impactful lessons you'll take away from this book. But before you skip, just know that understanding these fundamental metrics is a major step in becoming a healthcare entrepreneur instead of a dentist that owns a practice.

Gross Production

Production is one of the most important KPIs for dental practices because it measures the total amount of dentistry you perform on your base fee schedule before insurance adjustments, discounts, and write-offs. This metric gives you a clear picture of how well you're handling treatments, managing capacity, and using your resources. By keeping an eye on production, you can spot areas where you can boost productivity and efficiency. It also gives you a good sense of your overall financial health. If you don't track production, you might miss out on spotting inefficiencies and growth opportunities, which could lead to underutilized resources and potential revenue loss.

Recommended value: Variable

Gross production is a largely variable KPI. It is influenced by several factors. When working with clients, the first two ways to improve gross production are to increase new patient flow through modifying advertising budget and strategy and to look at case acceptance rate. Increasing new patients and increasing case acceptance rate quickly increases gross production. One client I've worked with was producing $40,000 per month—with this approach, we were able to double that number in four months.

Net Production

This is a crucial KPI that measures the total amount of money generated by providing dental services to patients. It's calculated with the following formula:

**Net Production =
Gross Production - Insurance Adjustments - Discounts - Write-Offs**

In essence, net production is the actual amount of money you expect to get paid for the dentistry you've provided in any given time period. This is an essential metric, as it helps you assess your practice's profitability and growth potential. By tracking it you can identify trends, compare performance over time, and make informed decisions about business strategy.

For example, many dentists experience a drop in net production during September—so much so that many refer to it as Sucktember. If you're tracking your metrics and notice that every year there's a 20 percent drop in net production during the month of September, you can then take some actions to alleviate that. You could increase your advertising budget at the end of June and July to drive more patients in during September. You could offer incentives to current patients for elective care like Invisalign or veneers. Or maybe you'd rather just take some time off, and you could schedule more efficiently during that month in order to do that. These are the types of decisions you can make when you have a good grip on your metrics.

Recommended value: As close to gross production as possible

The difference between gross and net production shows how much dentistry you are giving away. When I started my practice, my net production was 61 percent of my gross production. I was giving away 39 percent of my revenue through my in-network relationships with insurance, discount plans, and my in-house dental membership plan. This was in part because of unfavorable contracts with dental insurance companies along with an overly generous in-house dental membership plan.

I've since negotiated better contracts, reduced the amount of discounts I offer, and reduced my dependence on insurance contracts. (I've gone out of network with most insurance companies.) These strategies have brought that number significantly up. By doing this, I get to produce less dentistry and take more money home. If you're an in-network provider with several dental insurance companies, I highly recommend forming a strategy to improve your reimbursements and/or reduce your dependence on dental insurance for patient flow, as both of these will increase your net production. This process can be complicated and there are some risks involved. That's why I highly recommend working through it with a coach and/or insurance optimization specialist. Feel free to reach out at drbenfriberg.com for recommendations.

Collections

Collections are the lifeblood of a dental practice, measuring the amount of money collected from patients and insurance companies. This KPI is essential for tracking the practice's cash flow, monitoring payment trends, and ensuring the practice is paid for services rendered. Tracking collections allows dental practices to pinpoint issues with billing and collection processes and take corrective action to improve their finances. Without tracking collections, you could face cash flow issues, delayed payments, and unresolved billing problems, which can negatively impact the financial stability of your practice.

> **Recommended Value:** Enough to obtain the profit you need to sustain the lifestyle you desire

This number is a major indicator of practice health. If you want to improve it, you'll need to look at things like new patient acquisition, treatment plan amount, case acceptance, scheduling and confirmations, and your collection system. If you struggle to grow your collections to meet your goals, or they're trending in the wrong direction, then it's time to hire an outside resource to work with you on finding weak spots and creating a strategy to overcome those challenges.

Collections per Hour

Collections per hour measures the amount of money collected by the practice for every hour of operation. Like the collections KPI, this metric provides insights into the efficiency of your billing and collection processes, scheduling efficiency, and provider efficiency, and it can be used to predict the overall financial performance of your practice. By tracking collections per hour, you can identify peak times for revenue generation, optimize your scheduling and billing practices, and ensure your practice is maximizing its financial potential. If you don't track collections per hour, you might miss out on understanding the efficiency of your schedule and all the upstream opportunities that lead to a highly efficient seven-figure practice.

Recommended Value: This is a calculation-based goal.

Formula: Collections goal / number of scheduled days / hours per day

Example: If your goal is to collect $1,500,000 and take seven weeks off per year, and you're scheduled chairside seven hours per day, then your formula would look like this:

$1,500,000 / 168 days / 7 hours = $1,275 per hour

You should know this number. Your team should know this number. You should schedule your days to always hit this number, which equates to $8,930 per day minimum. It's important that your daily goal *exceeds* this number and that everyone is held accountable daily to hit it. It should be reviewed in the morning huddle, and the team should take an active role in creating opportunities to hit it.

If your collections per hour are low, you'll want to review your scheduling practices and look for ways to optimize them. You should be maximizing the amount of time you're doing dentistry while you're at the office. Consider block scheduling and quadrant-based dentistry if you haven't already—and if you aren't sure what those mean, that's something I can help you with in my one-on-one coaching.

Overhead

What does it cost to run your dental practice? Whatever that number is, that's your overhead. This is a KPI that measures the total expenses required to operate your practice and provides insights into the way you're spending money. Tracking overhead means you can identify areas where you can reduce expenses, optimize resource utilization, and enhance your practice's overall financial situation. If overhead isn't tracked, it will be difficult to control costs, leading to reduced profitability and financial strain on the practice. Overhead can—and absolutely should—be broken down further into sub-metrics. Your CPA should be able to provide you with a breakdown of major spending categories like wages, labs, marketing, and supplies as a percentage of collections. Tracking those sub-metrics then helps you further analyze where expenses can be reduced or optimized.

> **TIP:** There's a difference between a CPA that works with dentists and a dental CPA. You want to be working with the latter—someone who specializes in our industry. You can likely find a dental CPA with your own research, but I've included a few recommended CPA companies at the back of this book and on drbenfriberg.com/bookresources.

Recommended Value: 60 percent or less of total collections
Wages: 25 percent or less
Dental Supplies: 5 percent
Labs: Between 5–10 percent, depending on procedure mix (Lower indicates a possible issue with treatment planning. Higher indicates low collections or the need to find a more cost-effective lab.)

Increased cost of labor and materials have led to a significant rise in overhead for many dentists. Sixty-nine percent of dentists reported an increase in overhead in 2022. When this number is too high, the best way to manage it is to break down each major spending category into percentage of collections and strategize with your team and business coach on ways to reduce those numbers into the ideal range.

Profit Margin

This is why you're in business! If you were to only track one KPI, this is the one. Profit is simply the amount of money left over after all expenses have been paid. At the end of the day, it's the only KPI that matters. It's a measure of the practice's financial health and is essential for long-term sustainability. With this financial metric, you can determine if your dental practice is operating efficiently and make necessary adjustments to improve. Failing to monitor profit can result in unchecked expenses and missed opportunities to improve financial health, potentially jeopardizing the practice's sustainability.

Recommended Value: Greater than 40 percent of collections *(before doctor compensation)*

If your quarterly profit margin is consistently below 40 percent, there are significant areas for improvement. This metric is a lagging indicator of how well your practice is being run. Improving profit is a matter of improving collections and reducing costs. If your practice is below 40 percent profit, or if you don't know what your profit actually is, it's time for outside help.

Active Patients

Active patients are considered patients who have been seen in the past eighteen months or are currently on the schedule. It's a critical number to see how well you're retaining current patients and attracting new ones. By tracking this metric, you can identify trends that are impacting your practice. It will help you determine the downstream impact of business decisions like reducing insurance dependence or changing your advertising budget.

> **Recommended Value:** Variable, but typically between 1,200 and 2,000 per doctor

A high-end fee-for-service (FFS) practice requires fewer patients on average compared to an insurance-driven practice. When I was highly insurance dependent and had a large gross/net production difference, I averaged around 1,800 active patients. Now that I'm mostly FFS, my active patient numbers have dropped to 1,250. I have to see fewer patients and do less dentistry to collect the same amount. The number itself isn't that important; it's more about the trend. If your active patients metric is staying the same over time in a healthy range, it shows a healthy practice balance. If it's trending down without a known reason, then it's time to look at your retention strategies. If the number is steadily increasing, your retention strategy is effective. When the active patient number gets too large, it might be an opportunity to look at increasing practitioners and fees or reducing advertising budgets and insurance dependence to improve profitability.

New Patients Scheduled and Seen

This is a vital KPI. I consider it to be the second-most important after profit. It's simple: How many new patients have been seen this month and how many new patient appointments were scheduled yesterday? In my practice, we track this daily in the morning huddle. This metric offers valuable insights into the practice's external and internal marketing and advertising initiatives. Consistent tracking enables dental practices to pinpoint areas for improvement in their marketing strategies. Without tracking new patients, you might miss out on evaluating the effectiveness of your marketing strategies, leading to stagnation in patient growth. Ideally, you'll want to track both the number of new patients *and* where they came from (i.e., eight new patients from a Google Ads campaign, three from internal referrals). This will help keep your advertising company accountable and allow you to calculate your ROI from advertising efforts—something we'll discuss in chapter 8.

Recommended Value: 30–45 new patients per month

This range is for established practices that are not looking to achieve high growth. A FFS practice with great systems and high treatment plan acceptance will be on the lower end. An insurance-driven practice that struggles to achieve high treatment plan acceptance rates will need to be on the higher end. This KPI is a reflection of the impact of your internal and external advertising efforts as well as cyclical patterns in your community. There's also an element of new patient phone call conversion to be analyzed if this KPI is low. Your marketing efforts might be effective at getting the phone to ring, but a skill gap on the phone will lead to missed opportunities and wasted ad dollars.

Average Production per Patient (Annual Patient Value)

Average production per patient measures the average revenue produced by the practice per patient over a given time period, typically one year. This dental KPI is essential for assessing the practice's overall efficiency in scheduling, treatment planning, and speed of care. It's also useful for identifying opportunities for increasing revenue. If you're not tracking this metric, it will be difficult to know how effective your treatment planning and sales strategies are.

> **Recommended Value:** For a seven-figure practice, this number should be greater than $1,000 per patient.

The goal with this number is to always be improving. By tracking average production per patient, you can identify opportunities to enhance your services, improve treatment acceptance, and ultimately increase revenue. If your practice falls below this range, it might be worth evaluating your pricing models, treatment offerings, and patient engagement strategies to boost productivity. It can also show weaknesses in your recall and collections systems. In the end, the higher this metric is, the fewer patients you need to see to hit your goals.

Case Acceptance Rates

Case acceptance rates measure the percentage of patients who move forward and schedule treatment as planned. For example, if a patient comes in for a routine cleaning, and you identify that he has a cavity, does he actually schedule that appointment and go through with the recommended treatment? It's an incredibly important metric to prioritize.

This KPI informs you of potential problems around patients not committing to treatment and allows you to identify areas for improving team skills in communication and patient education. Case acceptance rate is very telling of your practice's overall performance. Put simply, if your case acceptance rate sucks, you have to work harder for everything. Your overhead will be higher because your collections will be down, you won't be getting good referrals, and you'll be spending more time for less money. Conversely, if your case acceptance rate is high, that means you aren't going to have to work as hard to make money because your patients are consistently going through with the additional treatment you're recommending. Without tracking case acceptance rates, you might struggle to understand why patients decline treatments, leading to lower acceptance rates and reduced revenue.

Recommended Value: 90 percent

Exceptional practices have created systems that allow them to communicate confidence and value as well as remove as many barriers to care as possible to achieve this goal. There will always be patients who don't accept care. Dentist hoppers and price shoppers won't commit. This isn't an excuse, though, to blow off opportunities to improve your systems. Having a goal of 90 percent creates a sharp focus for you and your team to always be improving and analyzing missed opportunities.

Cancellation or No-Show Rate

The percentage of cancellations and no-shows KPI helps you check your scheduling practices. This KPI provides insights into patient behavior, appointment scheduling systems, and patient commitment to treatment. If you notice a high no-show rate, it might be time to revisit your reminder systems or patient communication strategies. Failing to track this metric can result in high no-show rates, inefficient scheduling, and decreased patient engagement, ultimately affecting the practice's productivity and revenue.

Recommended Value: Always trending lower—5 percent or less is high-performing, and 10 percent or less is average

Since the Covid-19 pandemic, there's been a doubling of no-shows and cancellations in the dental field. Report after report shows this increase. With $700 per hour in collections for the dentist, a single no-show per day equates to approximately $125,000 in lost revenue per year! Keeping a close eye on this number is crucial to maximizing your schedule. Strategize your scheduling policy to include deposits, a robust confirmation system, and a strict no-show policy to reduce this number.

Hygiene Chair Utilization

Simply put, how many hours were your hygienists scheduled, and how many appointments were completed? This metric helps expose weaknesses in scheduling, follow-ups, and hygienist efficiency. If you fail to track this, you might miss out on understanding patient engagement levels and the effectiveness of your preventive care, potentially leading to lower patient satisfaction and missed revenue opportunities.

Recommended Value: Trending toward 100 percent

In an ideal world your hygiene team will be busy all day every day. When this number is low, it shows weaknesses in your recall system, confirmation system, and patient education systems. It can also be a result of low new patient flow, overstaffing, or hygienists who aren't fulfilling their responsibilities in managing time effectively, such as booking sixty minutes for appointments that only require thirty to forty minutes.

Getting Started

At this point, you may be feeling a bit overwhelmed by all these metrics. That's completely normal. The key isn't to try implementing everything at once, but rather to start building the habit of regularly reviewing your practice's performance metrics.

The first step is to ensure you have easy access to this information—either by creating your own tracking system or investing in one of the many software solutions that provide this data in an easy-to-digest dashboard format.

Once you have access to the data, schedule dedicated time each week to review your key metrics. This could be as simple as spending twenty to thirty minutes every Monday morning, looking at the previous week's performance—your production, collections, case acceptance rate, new patients, and other critical KPIs. At the end of each month, review your profit and loss statement to get the full financial picture. The important thing is making this review a consistent part of your routine.

This is where you truly start operating like a healthcare entrepreneur rather than just a dentist who owns a practice. The founder of modern management theory, Peter Drucker, is often quoted as saying, "What gets measured gets managed." By understanding your numbers and regularly monitoring your metrics, you can make informed decisions about which levers to pull to drive your practice forward. Rather than simply trying to out-produce your costs, you can strategically identify opportunities for improvement and growth. Start measuring what matters most for your practice's success.

Define, Refine, Implement

Define: Determine the information you need to track and make sure you have access to it.

Refine: Schedule time in your calendar to routinely review your metrics.

Implement: Stay committed to that time for review and use it intentionally—don't just look at the metrics, but use them to inform your decisions.

Part Three

MARKETING

YOU ARE THE CMO

Practically everything we've covered up to this point is dependent on one thing: *acquiring new patients.* Your business systems? Not very useful if you don't have patients. Team culture? If you can't pay your team, you're going to have much bigger problems on your hands. Practice mission? Not going to achieve it if no one's coming into your office. Personal vision? You guessed it. While money isn't everything, I think you'll need a steady source of income to build your ideal life and practice.

Nearly every business needs to market itself to grow. And if you think you don't need marketing because people "need" to go to a dentist, well, that mentality is certainly not going to get you to seven figures. The reality is that half the population doesn't attend a dentist regularly, so the idea that people will come to you because they "need" to is simply not true. Those people either don't care, have financial concerns, or think their dental health is good enough to not require regular dental appointments.

With the right marketing, you can reach those people, change their minds, and get them into your dental practice. And if you don't do it, another dentist will. There are seventeen dentists within a one-mile radius of my office. I can't just hang back and wait for people to come to me, because they'll just go to one of those other seventeen dentists. This is obviously location-dependent—I do have a few clients who are the only dentists in their area and already have more than enough clientele. They don't advertise. But they still have a brand, and they still use internal marketing techniques to keep their customers coming back—all of which we'll be covering in the following chapters. (Plus, they'll be ready to start advertising as soon as another dentist sets up shop in their area.)

Moral of the story: If you want to compete, grow your business, and reach seven figures, you need to be using marketing and advertising. But what many dentists and business owners get wrong is they focus on marketing before setting up the right foundation. There's a reason why we covered leadership and management before marketing. Mastering leadership and management *before* accelerating your marketing efforts will make your marketing far more successful. Leadership and management are requirements for growth. If you were to heavily market your business before tackling those critical areas, you'd be hindering yourself by bringing people into a broken, inefficient, and misguided system. And we don't want that.

So now that you've got the foundation, it's time to kick things up a notch by increasing the flow of new patients. How are we going to do that? Well, through marketing of course. Which starts with *you*.

You Can't Outsource This

One of the most common problems I encounter with healthcare entrepreneurs is that they don't take personal responsibility for their marketing and patient acquisition. They believe that they can hire an agency or consultant and outsource that responsibility to them entirely. If there's a problem with marketing, it's not the owner's fault; it's the agency's fault! Fire them! Find someone new!

I can't tell you how many times I've had a practice owner tell me, "My marketing company just isn't working. I think I need to fire them." But when you're on your third, fourth, or fifth marketing company, you have to ask yourself: Is it really them? Or is it you? What's the common denominator?

Here's the thing. You, as the doctor, are the chief marketing officer of your business. You are solely responsible for driving new patients into your practice. Yes, you can outsource the marketing, but you can't outsource the responsibility. And until you realize this, your marketing will be either unsuccessful or not nearly as successful as it could be, regardless of how many marketing agencies you hire (or fire).

Last year, I implemented a ton of advertising techniques with my marketing company. I tried television ads, radio ads, YouTube, Spotify, Google Ads, Meta—if you can spend money on it, I did. And it worked. I was getting sixty to seventy new patients every month, and it actually was going so well that I couldn't keep up. I was overbooked. I was having to schedule patients four months out, which isn't a good situation because those patients are going to go somewhere else.

So I called my marketing company and told them to stop the ads. I needed time to get caught up. Eventually, I did, and then the second quarter ended up being the worst I'd had in four years. That's because after I got caught up, I didn't have any new patient generators to bring revenue into my business. So I called up my marketing company again and told them to ramp things up. They got back to me, saying it would take about four weeks to start seeing results. It wasn't until June of that year that I really saw any progress.

Ultimately, that was my mistake—I'd thought I could "set and forget" my marketing. I wasn't monitoring how many new patients were coming in. I was busy working with patients every day! That stuff just wasn't on my mind. But if I'd been a bit more involved in the process, I could've avoided that whole situation. I would've noticed the drop in new patients and talked to my marketing company far earlier so we could proactively develop a plan to get things back on track. That's why I now have a system where my team tells me every single day how many new patients we've scheduled and how many we've seen that month. So when I see that number start to dip, I know I have to call up my marketing company and get things moving.

Marketing is the lifeblood of your business. It's simply too important to delegate completely—no matter how much you'd like to. At the end of the day, no one will care as much about your business as you do. These are *your* goals. This practice is part of *your* vision. You can't just give away one of the most important levers in your business and expect that person or entity to achieve the exact results you're looking for. That would be bad leadership.

And keep in mind: *you're a doctor.* You stand for more than just any other business. You're a community leader. You take care of people's health. That needs to come through in your marketing, which isn't something most marketing companies are going to be aware of.

I'm not saying you need to be an expert marketer. You can and should hire professionals to help you with your brand. They can advise you, create content, run ads, and do all the nitty-gritty stuff. You really just need to be willing and ready to get involved. That means giving them direction. It means knowing *enough* about marketing to gauge whether they're doing a good job. And most importantly, it means incorporating your own personality into your marketing. Remember, it's your practice! That also means it's your marketing! Act accordingly.

Internal and External Marketing

Before we get into the how-to, let's clarify some terms. At a high level, *marketing* is the overall strategy of how you communicate your business to your community. It's the total strategy of a patient's first contact with you all the way through their patient experience. I tell my clients to think of it "from the first call to the five-star review." Everything the patient experiences is part of your marketing. Then within marketing, you have specific tactics like advertising, partnerships, reviews, and even your financial policies—we'll be diving into all of these in chapter 10.

I like to break marketing down into two big categories: internal marketing and external marketing. *Internal marketing* is about what you can do *inside* your business to both retain current patients and generate new patients. For a dentist, most of your internal marketing efforts revolve around patient experience. How can you provide such a great experience that your patient wants to come back, tell their friends how great you are, and write a review online? This stuff is powerful and will shape the way your community perceives you. It's also typically low-cost, which makes it a great place to start.

External marketing is about what you can do *outside* of your business to generate new patients that are not connected to your practice in any way. There's typically going to be a direct cost here—you're largely exchanging dollars for visibility. Most of the traditional marketing tactics you're familiar with fall within external marketing: advertising, media coverage, social media, nonprofit partnerships, networking, and so forth.

Now, I highly suggest you don't try to implement external advertising on your own or through your brother's wife's cousin who "does marketing on the side." After helping develop the marketing strategy for hundreds of dental practices, I've seen what works and what doesn't—and your brother's wife's cousin doesn't work. The stakes are too high. Don't risk the success of your practice to save a few bucks, because I can guarantee it will cost you way more in the long run. External marketing is an investment, not a cost to be managed.

This is another one of those situations where you can't have one or the other—you need both. Internal and external marketing support each other. External marketing brings new patients in while internal marketing keeps them there. Some external marketing efforts also support internal marketing, and vice versa. If you want to build a seven-figure practice, you really need to focus on both. I'll show you *exactly* how to do that in chapter 9, where we'll be going in-depth on all of the specific internal and external marketing tactics you should be considering.

The Art and Science

I'm just going to come right out and say it: I like marketing. And one reason I like marketing is because there's an art and a science to it. The logical side of my brain loves analyzing the performance of a new advertisement and getting into the nitty-gritty metrics around ad spend, impressions, and how those things are affecting our bottom line. But I also love the creative side. I get to instill my own personality into my brand and my marketing, and that's actually pretty fun. (I know, I know. Marketing? Fun? Yes, you too may come to enjoy it.)

The science of marketing is really the science of influence. There's no doubt about it—at its core, marketing works. Microeconomics is an entire study around how rational individuals respond to incentives in the free market. When you market your business, you're communicating that incentive to your audience. This might be a literal incentive, like a discount for new patients or a free toothbrush at every cleaning; or it might be not so literal, as in, "Come see us because if you don't, bad things will happen to your oral health—and that's not good!"

All of the science behind how human beings make decisions and gain influence can be boiled down to the simple concept of alleviating pain and pursuing pleasure. Those are the incentives. When you're working on your marketing, you should always have this in the back of your mind. A new patient special, for example, is alleviating the financial pain of going to the dentist. At my practice, we try to offer same-day care whenever possible. We're literally telling our audience that if you're in pain, you can come in today and have that pain alleviated.

There's also the numbers side of marketing—making sure the revenue your marketing efforts are generating is greater than the expense and looking at the metrics behind your ads to figure out what's working and what isn't. The "science" of how digital marketing works in this day and age can get pretty complex. Personally, I like diving into this stuff, but if you don't, that's okay. As long as you understand the fundamentals, you'll be able to leave many of the finer details to your marketing company.

If you're not into the numbers, you may be more drawn to what I think of as the "art" of marketing. Just like I can change the decorations in my office to feel more authentic to me, I can use language and imagery in my advertising that's authentic to me and my brand. I can put out social posts or run advertisements in ways that *I want*. And that can be fun. (It's also incredibly effective, which you'll learn more about when we get into your marketing avatar.)

Marketing is incredibly nuanced, and there are certain aspects that simply can't be boiled down into hard data. It's trial and error. It's thinking creatively and coming up with a new idea for an ad that might work or might not. It's looking at a social post from your team and saying, "This is awesome, but what if we tweaked this little part? Does that feel better?" Even with all the science and metrics you have at your disposal, at the end of the day, there's no certainty in marketing.

Now, this does pose a slight problem. As dentists, we're very scientific people. We want everything to be defined and predictable. If I use the cement with the right instructions, it will never come off. If I use this marketing tactic in this way, it will never fail. Unfortunately, that's not how marketing works—and that's something you'll have to accept as a business owner.

Sometimes you'll spend one dollar and get ten back. Sometimes you'll spend one dollar and get a hundred back. And sometimes you'll spend a hundred dollars and get nothing back. That's the way it goes. It doesn't mean marketing is ineffective or bad—it just means you need to be comfortable with testing new things and getting creative. The good news is that when you combine the art and science of marketing, you begin to lower that level of uncertainty to the point where, if done right, you can be confident that your marketing investment will pay off. But to do that, you need to be tracking your progress correctly.

> **TIP:** Don't underestimate what the art of marketing can do for your business—both monetarily and in terms of personal fulfillment. Marketing your business in a way that is uniquely you is typically a far more effective strategy than trying to endlessly manipulate some algorithm to your advantage. Plus, it's easier, feels less "salesy," and can even be kinda fun!

Budget, Tracking, and ROI

A mentor of mine, Jayme Amos, has a quote that has helped me and hundreds of dentists understand the fundamentals of tracking marketing: "If you don't track your marketing, it isn't an investment. It's a donation." For the long-term health of your practice, it's vital that you understand three things related to your marketing:

1. How much money to spend
2. How to determine if a marketing tactic is money or time well spent
3. How effective the tactic is at meeting your goals

Without a budget and without a system to track how impactful your marketing is, there's no way to improve it. There's no way to know whether the time and money you're spending on marketing is useful or a complete waste. Creating a budget, tracking progress, and analyzing its impact on your profitability *is* your most important responsibility as the CMO of your practice.

Budget

Before you can create a budget, you need to clarify your goals around the growth of your practice. Your goals will significantly impact your budget. Now, you should already have a good idea of what your goals are from your practice vision and mission—if not, this is a good time to think back and consider what you'll need to have happen in the next one to three years to move closer to your vision. Are you looking for fast growth, expansion of providers, and increased collections? Or are you looking at becoming highly efficient with lean operations that drive high profit?

The marketing budget is going to look very different between these two goals. To get you started, here are a few industry benchmarks you should be aware of, which I've broken down based on the status and goals of the practice. These percentages are based on desired growth and collections—not current. For example, if you want to grow to be a $1,500,000 practice and are at $860,000 now, you can expect to spend close to $10,000 per month, or 8-9 percent of your target revenue, on marketing efforts.

Established practice:

- Maintain current collections: 3-5 percent of annual collections
- Increase collections: 6-8 percent
- Rapid growth and practice expansion: greater than 9 percent of goal collections

New or struggling practice:

- Maintain current collections: 6-7 percent of annual collections
- Increase collections: 8-9 percent
- Rapid growth and practice expansion: greater than 10 percent of goal collections

Keep in mind that these figures are just starting points—the real numbers will be highly variable based on individual practice specifics. For instance, if you're a start-up in a highly competitive market, you could expect to be on the higher end of each range depending on your goals. If you're the only dentist in a twenty-mile radius, then your advertising budget might be significantly less and only targeted to drive large specialty cases like Invisalign or implants to your practice.

The budget you set is also dependent on the advice of your marketing company. They'll help guide this process based on their experience in similar markets and similar practices. As the CMO, it's your responsibility to hold your marketing company accountable to the budget you set and the results they say are possible. Make sure your goal for new patients per month, the type of patients you want, and the procedures you enjoy are shared openly and often so they can manage and adapt their strategy to hit your goals.

Your budget isn't a "set it and forget it" line item on your to-do list. It's more akin to a throttle you're constantly adjusting to make sure you're on the right track to hit your goals. If your practice is always slow in September (or Sucktember, as mentioned previously), it would be wise to step on the gas pedal and increase your budget in June and July to drive production into September. If you have a year-end rush and you can't find an empty chair for a patient in all of December every year, then don't spend a bunch on advertising in November.

Tracking

Remember, what gets measured gets managed—and this holds true for your marketing. As the manager of your marketing, you *must* track your results. But how? It's really quite simple. When your phone rings and a patient says they want to set up an appointment as a new patient, your team responds every single time with this: "That's so great to hear! How did you first hear about our practice?" Then they record that in your practice management software.

When you start measuring this, you'll quickly be able to determine if your marketing is working.

Once this information has been tracked for several months, it's possible to set up better analysis of the effectiveness of your marketing campaigns. As a general rule, any campaign—whether it's Google Ads, mailers, or Meta—requires at least three months of data before you can determine its effectiveness. Many doctors I've worked with have jumped from marketing company to marketing company after only a few months! I know some practices who are on their fifth marketing company in less than five years. That's crazy. In many cases, the owner of these dental practices had unreasonable expectations (sometimes at the fault of the marketing company's sales team) and didn't have patience to allow the advertising to work.

The simple "How did you hear about us?" tracking system is very effective when executed well and consistently. There is, however, a new wave of tracking systems available at several different dental marketing agencies. These systems will plug into your practice management software like Open Dental or Dentrix. A good marketing company will be able to use software to track your ad campaigns, phone calls, schedule, production, and collections based on a patient's actions online. For instance, a patient searches "dentist near me" and they click on your ad, call, and make an appointment. Then, two weeks later, they complete a crown in your office. This software will be able to connect the ad spend on Google to the specific procedure they received. (I know, kind of scary—but also helpful!)

This level of sophistication makes tracking the efficacy of your advertising much more transparent so you can move away from "I feel like it's working" to knowing exactly what's working and how. If this level of sophistication is important to you, then it might be worth asking your marketing company if they're able to implement something like that.

So, now that we've established the importance of tracking our marketing and advertising, it's time to manage them! A major component of managing your marketing and advertising is calculating return on investment (ROI) and maximizing your spending to achieve ever higher results.

Return on Investment

First off, understanding the ROI of your marketing efforts is crucial. It helps you see what's really working and what's just throwing sand into the wind. Without this calculation, you could be pouring money into ads that don't bring new patients. By calculating ROI, you ensure every dollar spent actually helps grow your practice.

Calculating ROI isn't as daunting as it sounds. You can use this formula to track the ROI of specific campaigns as well as the ROI of all your marketing efforts combined. I'd recommend focusing on specific campaigns so you can start to determine which ones are working and which aren't. The formula looks like this:

You'll start by figuring out the total revenue your marketing efforts have generated. And when I say "total," that includes new patients and any additional services they've opted for because of your campaigns. Next, subtract the total cost of these marketing efforts. Keep in mind, this isn't just ad spend but also labor and other related costs. Finally, divide this net profit by the total marketing costs and multiply by 100 to get your ROI percentage.

For example, if I spend $500 on a Meta campaign and it generates $6000 in collections for my practice, I would calculate ROI as such:

This comes out to an ROI of 1,100 percent. You can also think of it as a ratio of 11:1. So that means for every dollar I invested in that campaign I got $11 back in collections. (Not bad!)

Once you've got your ROI, you can make smarter decisions. In general, we look for at least a 5:1 ROI in dentistry. If a campaign has an ROI of 5:1 or more, it's a keeper—maybe even something to double down on. If a campaign flops, it's time to rethink or scrap it. This way, you're not just throwing spaghetti at the wall to see what sticks; you're strategically investing in what works. As you're tracking your ROI, you will also likely find a point of saturation for your efforts.

Saturation comes when you have taken full advantage of a specific marketing tactic, for instance Meta ads. They might have had an amazing ROI at a budget of $500/month, so you double down and go to $1,000 per month. Now your chairs are filling up and your schedule is looking good, but you want even more! So you go to a $1,500 per month budget. The number of new patients doesn't go up and your collections don't change, so your ROI will actually dip on your Meta ads at this point. You have reached a saturation point where more money doesn't increase results for a given tactic. This information is vital to tell your marketing agency so they can either create a new campaign or modify the current one.

Without understanding and setting a budget, tracking the results, and calculating ROI, you could be donating $6,000 per year to Meta and never know it. You'll want to make ROI tracking a regular habit. (I'd recommend dedicating some time to this on every one of your admin days!) Continuously monitoring your efforts helps you stay agile and responsive. You'll spot trends and adapt more quickly, ensuring your practice always benefits from the best possible strategies. Plus, keeping a close eye on ROI helps you set more realistic and informed marketing goals for the future. Keep in mind that you're accountable for the results of your marketing—but you're also in full control. Act accordingly!

> **TIP:** Any good marketing company should be able to provide you this data, so don't feel like you need to be manually calculating everything yourself. But knowing the basics of how it works is important! Later, we'll discuss how to vet marketing companies and find one that works for you.

Fundamentals of Brand Identity

There's an old saying in marketing: "When you try to appeal to everyone, you appeal to no one." And it's true. By targeting a specific audience or even a specific type of person, you'll appeal directly to that person, and they'll be so attracted to what you're doing that they'll take action. If you try to appeal to everyone, however, your message lands flat.

It's a bit counterintuitive. If you're just marketing to one type of person, you might think you're limiting yourself. Well, the short answer is that you're not, and here's why.

My brother is a real estate coach. He works with real estate agents, insurance brokers, and the like, helping them improve their real estate business, generate more revenue, etc. At one point, he had two clients who stood out from all the other people he was working with. One of them was a gun-toting, truck-driving, outspoken Republican. The other was the exact opposite—just about as liberal as you could get, bordering on "tree-hugger" territory. Definitely drove a Subaru or a Prius.

Now, you might think these people wouldn't make for great realtors because they'd put off a lot of people. But the one thing they had in common was that they both had a line out the door of people who wanted to work with them. They were *wildly* successful, more so than the vast majority of his other clients who came off as totally normal, middle-of-the-road realtors.

Why did this happen? *Because people want to work with people they identify with.* So all the gun-toting Republicans instantly wanted to work with the first guy, and all the liberals wanted to work with the second guy. And it makes sense. Who would you rather work with, the red shirt and khaki realtor, or the person who dresses like you, has the same opinions as you, and thinks like you? It's a no-brainer.

As dentists, it's the same thing. You have to be *you*. When you express yourself authentically in your marketing, your message will connect with people like you. And the result is that your marketing efforts won't only be more effective, but you'll also attract the exact type of people you want to work with. Better yet, it's infinitely easier to just be yourself to try to put on some facade and act like someone you're not. It's a win-win.

And here's the other thing to consider. The average solo practitioner only needs around 1,500 to 2,000 patients to run a successful seven-figure practice. Unless you're truly located in the middle of nowhere, you can find 1,500 to 2,000 people that are like you and resonate with your unique personality. When you create a brand that's authentically you—that's reflective of who you are as a person—you'll naturally attract those people. It took me way too long to realize this, but once I did, it was like the greatest hack I'd ever discovered. *You mean to tell me that just being myself will improve my marketing efforts, and I'll get to work with people I actually like hanging out with?* Yes, past Ben. Yes, I do.

But it gets even better. If you think about it, there's even another level to consider. When I work with people who I actually like and would want to hang out with in my spare time, we end up building a great rapport. I have real relationships with my patients. I do actually hang out with many of them in my spare time! And I love it! That relationship and rapport builds trust and provides a great patient experience. Which means they're going to come back to me for a long, long time. They're happy and I'm happy.

Part of your job as the CMO is to show up as your authentic self in your marketing. This also goes back to the fact that *it's your practice*! For example, I like wearing bow ties, and I like dogs. I wear a bow tie every day at work, and there's a dog in our office. That's my brand. I'm the bow-tie dentist with the dog, and I attract people who are into that.

Everything about you, your team, your office—even the way it smells, sounds, and feels—is part of your brand. Put simply, the more you can make it your own, the better. Take music, for example. I remember when I first started out, I had a consultant tell me I should play mellow, generic music that would appeal to most people. I said, "Screw that!" (Not to his face, but you get the idea.) I mean, I also have to listen to that music every day—in fact, I listen to it for way more time than my patients do! So if I'm going to listen to it all day, I'm going to listen to what I want to listen to. In my practice, we listen to tons of great music: Vampire Weekend, The Head and the Heart, ZZ Top. We even have '80s day. I love it, and the people who like that type of music are psyched that they don't have to listen to elevator music while they get their teeth cleaned.

So, with all this in mind, how do you actually make this happen? How do you clarify your brand identity? And how do you convey that to your team and marketing company? The easiest way to do *all* of this is by creating an avatar.

Your Avatar

In marketing, your avatar is the type of person you want to reach and attract to your business. It's your ideal client—or in our case, ideal patient. Clarifying who that person is will allow you to then focus all your marketing efforts toward them. When you're working with a marketing company, your avatar also becomes an essential tool to educate them on how your marketing should look and feel.

The most important lesson I can teach you about your avatar is that it should be incredibly specific. The biggest mistake business owners make when doing an exercise like this is that they use a range of people or a type of person instead of focusing on *one specific person*. You've probably heard people talk about avatars as a wide swath of people, like "young males between the ages of eighteen and thirty who like sports." In my mind, that's not an avatar. It's far too general. We already know that the more specific we can be with our marketing, the better, and your avatar is what will provide that specificity.

I have one avatar for my dental practice and one for my mastermind, since those are two very different types of people. The avatar for my dental practice is Julie. Julie is sixty years old, retired, and interested in prioritizing her well-being. I could tell you practically everything you could know about Julie because I've written it down in meticulous detail. Here's what that actually looks like (I've included a template that you can use for this at the end of the chapter):

Thrive Family Dental Marketing Avatar

Personal:

Name: Julie
Age: 60
Location: Recently relocated to the area (from New England)
Occupation: Retired
Family: Children graduated from college, no longer living at home
Marital Status: Married (husband is also retired)

Demographics and Background:

- **Life Stage:** Newly retired and looking forward to this exciting new chapter in life
- **Relocation:** Recently moved to the area after retirement to enjoy a warmer climate, be closer to new opportunities, and embrace her love for outdoor activities
- **Education:** College-educated, with an interest in maintaining a sharp mind and healthy body
- **Income:** Comfortable retirement income, looking to invest in health and wellness

Lifestyle and Interests:

- **Health Focus:** Julie is motivated to start taking better care of herself now that she has more time and freedom. She's eager to prioritize her well-being, including dental health, since she has more time to invest in her appearance and health now.
- **Outdoor Enthusiast:** She loves being outside, whether it's taking walks with her dog, enjoying local parks, hiking, or gardening in her new home.

- **Pets:** She is a dog lover, and her dog is a big part of her daily routine. She enjoys taking long walks with her pet and visits local dog parks regularly.
- **Social and Community-Oriented:** Julie enjoys making new connections and is excited to be part of her new community. She is active in local events, whether through meet-ups or volunteering at community centers.

Pain Points:

- **Dental Health Concerns:** After retirement, Julie has started thinking more about preventative health, including dental care, which she may have neglected while raising her children and working. She's looking for a dental practice that offers comprehensive care, focusing on preventive treatment and improving her overall health.
- **Transition and Change:** Julie is still adjusting to the transition to retirement, which includes finding local services and health care professionals that feel like a "good fit" for her lifestyle.
- **Anxiety with Dental Procedures:** She has had bad experiences in the past and has anxiety toward dentistry that she is looking to overcome. She wants a dentist that will take time to discuss treatment and is nonjudgmental of her apprehension toward dental work.

Goals:

- **Healthier Smile:** Julie wants to take control of her health, starting with her smile. She's concerned about the effects of aging on her teeth and is looking for a friendly dental practice to help her maintain healthy teeth and gums.
- **Self-Care:** As she embarks on a journey to invest in her health, she seeks providers who can help her build healthy habits that she can maintain long-term.

- **Community Connection:** Julie wants a dentist who values community and fosters an environment where she feels comfortable and welcome.

Messaging for Julie:
- **Voice/Tone:** Warm, compassionate, and trustworthy

As you can see, this is far more than a simple demographic. By homing in on who Julie is as a person, I can then easily market my business to that specific person. Not all my patients are female, and they're not all sixty years old, but most of them are fairly similar to Julie because they resonate with the messaging that I'm putting out in the world.

If you're skeptical, just look at the avatar for my dental mastermind, Bryan. Bryan is a thirty-eight-year-old dentist who's owned his private practice for less than five years and is feeling overwhelmed. He's married, has two children who are under six years old, and feels like he isn't mentally or emotionally present with them when he's home. He tries to prioritize his time with family, but it's a struggle.

For Bryan, dentistry isn't as fun as it used to be, and he sometimes dreads the thought of seeing another patient or picking up a drill. Too often, he asks himself, "Can I really do this for the rest of my career?" Here's a little more information about Bryan:
- Through the process of becoming a dentist and a practice owner, he has lost touch with his hobbies and pastimes that used to make him feel alive.
- He is a former athlete who has always enjoyed moving and exercising but hasn't made it a priority because of all the other demands in his life.
- His dental practice and his staff seem to run him, and there is a seemingly endless amount of work to get done.
- The practice is doing okay but not meeting his goals. He knows they could have more revenue and more profit, but he is unsure of the steps on how to get there.

- He is dedicated to his family and patients but feels like there is something missing, that he doesn't have control over his circumstances.
- He is ready for change.

Sound familiar? If you picked up this book and have made it this far, I'd be willing to bet some, if not most, of those bullet points resonate with you. That's not a coincidence. It's because I wrote this book for Bryan and I marketed it to Bryan. Everything I do in my mastermind—the branding, the content, the emails, the website—is all for Bryan. You might not be thirty-eight years old, you might not be male, and you might not be a former athlete, but you share enough similarities with Bryan that you were drawn to this book.

> **TIP:** Yes, Bryan is very similar to the young Ben Friberg you learned about in the introduction. It's very common for your avatar to be a reflection of yourself. That's okay! Lean into it. It makes perfect sense that you'd want to work with people similar to you.

The more focused you are with your avatar, the more effective it will be. You should know your avatar as well as you know your best friend. When you have that level of clarity and understanding, your avatar then becomes a tool which you can use to guide your marketing. If you're wondering what to write for a social media post, you can ask yourself, "What would my avatar want to see?" If your marketing company brings you multiple versions of an ad, you can just ask yourself which one your avatar would like the most. And when your team knows your avatar just as well as you do, they can answer those questions for you. That's not possible when your avatar is a range of people between the ages of thirty and fifty.

When everyone at your marketing company understands your avatar, they can speak in ways that will resonate with them, entice them, meet their pain points, and solve their problems. Without that focus, you're just guessing and hoping that you'll find the right person. That means you're spending more money to get fewer people. A specific avatar makes your marketing easier, more effective, and gives you the best possible ROI.

I've already given you a lot of responsibilities as the CMO of your business, and I'm going to give you two more (then we'll be done, I swear). As the CMO, it's your responsibility to clearly define your avatar, document exactly who that person is, and share that with your team. Your brand and all your marketing efforts should then be designed to resonate with that specific person. On the following page, I've included an exercise to help you get started on this.

A Note on Brand Guides

Your avatar is just one piece of your brand, although it's a significant one. Ideally, you should have a "brand guide" for your business that encapsulates nearly everything someone might need to know about your brand—from your avatar to your logo, the hex codes for your branding colors, words you like and don't like to use on social media, etc.

Creating a brand guide can be a very time-intensive process, and it should always be a work in progress. As you clarify more parts of your brand, those details get added to your brand guide, and it serves as the one source of truth for you and your marketing company. It should clarify exactly how your marketing looks and feels.

I could probably write an entire book about how to build a brand guide, and there are surely many of those out there. However, this isn't something I'd recommend you spend time on—rather, it's something your marketing company should be handling for you. If your marketing company doesn't already have a brand guide for you, I'd recommend asking them to get started. Your avatar can be the first piece of that puzzle.

If your marketing company is hesitant about building this or doesn't seem to know what you're talking about, that's a big red flag. Brand guides are standard operating procedure for any marketing agency, regardless of industry. You should also have full ownership of it—it's *your* brand guide that they've created for you, not the other way around.

> **TIP:** Connecting with your avatar is a lot easier with digital advertising because you can actually target people based on their interests, age, and many other demographics. That means you can create an ad for your avatar and put it smack dab in front of the specific demographic they fall into. That's not possible with mass media like television, radio, or billboards, which is why I typically don't recommend those for dentists. The one exception is if you're in a small market and mass media is inexpensive.

AVATAR WORKSHEET

This worksheet is designed to help you create a clear and detailed profile of your ideal patient. A well-defined patient avatar will guide your marketing, advertising, and communication strategies, ensuring they resonate with the patients you want to attract.

1. **Demographics**
   - **Age:** (e.g., 30–45)
   - **Gender:** (e.g., female, male, nonbinary)
   - **Marital Status:** (e.g., single, married, divorced)
   - **Children:** (e.g., number of children and their ages)
   - **Occupation:** (e.g., engineer, teacher, entrepreneur)
   - **Income Level:** (e.g., $50,000–$100,000 annually)
   - **Location:** (e.g., suburban, urban, rural)

2. **Psychographics**
   - **Values and Beliefs:** (e.g., family-oriented, prioritizes health)
   - **Hobbies and Interests:** (e.g., fitness, traveling, reading)
   - **Lifestyle:** (e.g., busy professional, stay-at-home parent)
   - **Pain Points or Challenges:** (e.g., fear of dental visits, time constraints)

- **Health Priorities:** (e.g., preventive care, cosmetic improvements)

3. Dental History and Preferences
- **Frequency of Visits:** (e.g., regular, only in emergencies)
- **Past Dental Experiences:** (e.g., positive, negative, neutral)
- **Services of Interest:** (e.g., cosmetic dentistry, orthodontics, preventive care)
- **Preferred Communication Style:** (e.g., detailed explanations, quick summaries)

4. Goals and Aspirations
- **What are they hoping to achieve with dental care?** (e.g., whiter teeth, improved confidence, better oral health)
- **What are their long-term goals for oral health?** (e.g., maintaining a healthy smile into old age)

5. Marketing Insights
- **Where do they spend their time online?** (e.g., Facebook, Instagram, YouTube)
- **What type of content do they engage with?** (e.g., educational blogs, video tutorials)
- **Preferred Communication Channels:** (e.g., email, text, phone calls)
- **Local Community Engagement:** (e.g., school events, fitness centers, local charities)

6. Personal Narrative
Combine all the above insights into a brief story about your ideal patient. For example: "Our ideal patient is a thirty-five-year-old working mother of two who values family and health. She's busy balancing her career as a teacher and her family life but prioritizes preventive care to maintain her bright smile. She's active on Instagram and loves engaging with short, educational posts about health. She wants a dental office that understands her time constraints and offers flexible appointment options."

7. **Visual Representation**
   - **Optional:** Attach a stock image or sketch that represents your ideal patient.

Define, Refine, Implement

Define: Identify your role as the CMO of your business. What are your roles and responsibilities?

Refine: Create the systems to track, manage, and improve your marketing efforts.

Implement: Carve out time in your admin day to proactively work on your marketing efforts.

INTERNAL AND EXTERNAL MARKETING

Any time you're making a significant purchase or choosing a new service provider—whether it's finding a gym, selecting a financial advisor, or choosing a school for your kids—the process is usually the same. You might ask friends for recommendations, do some research online, check reviews, drive by, or stop in to get a feel for the place. Once you make a decision, you'll probably pay close attention during your initial visit or your first time using the product. If it doesn't feel right, maybe you'll look into alternatives. These decisions involve multiple touchpoints and careful consideration. For the average person, choosing a dentist is one of those decisions.

Understanding this journey is crucial to marketing your practice effectively. Every potential patient goes through a series of steps before they ever sit in your chair: becoming aware of your practice, considering whether to choose you, making the decision to book an appointment, and finally experiencing your care firsthand. Then, once they've experienced your care, they have to decide whether they'll return. In our case, this can be even more complicated since we may be recommending additional care, which means additional costs for them. Your marketing efforts need to support them at each step of this journey.

This chapter is going to be different from the others. While the previous ones focused heavily on mindset and concepts, we're now going to get tactical. We'll be diving into specific strategies and techniques you can implement in your practice immediately. Some of these might seem simple—and they are! But don't let their simplicity fool you. When implemented correctly and consistently, these techniques can transform your practice.

In the last chapter, we discussed the key differences between internal and external marketing. Now, I'll show you exactly how to use both channels to guide patients through their journey, from first hearing about your practice to becoming loyal, long-term patients who refer their friends and family. I'll provide specific, actionable steps for implementing each strategy, along with real examples from practices that have used them successfully.

Remember, the goal isn't just to attract more patients—it's to attract the right patients. By understanding the patient journey and implementing the strategies we'll cover, you can build a marketing system that consistently brings in patients who fall into the demographic of your avatar, which means they'll already be aligned with your values and appreciate the care you're providing. This will not only boost your revenue but also make your practice a much more enjoyable place to work for you and your team.

By the end of this chapter, you'll have a complete roadmap for marketing your practice effectively at every stage of the patient journey. It's a big one, so buckle up and consider keeping a notebook handy to jot down some ideas. And remember that you can always refer back to this later as needed.

We're going to start with internal marketing, as many of the tactics within it are low-cost and will improve your other marketing efforts. If you're just getting started with marketing your practice, you'll want to make sure you've checked off many, if not all, of these tactics before you move on to external marketing.

Internal Marketing: Fundamentals and Tactics

As we discussed in the last chapter, internal marketing is a crucial component of the success of any dental practice. These efforts focus on leveraging existing resources, such as current patients and staff, to promote the practice to your already existing patients with the goal of increasing current patient value (by turning them into lifelong customers), and attracting new patients (through referrals and word-of-mouth).

Internal marketing starts with the patient experience. By improving patient experience, you'll be able to predictably increase annual patient value and internally sourced referrals. When well-orchestrated, it will ultimately grow your practice and strengthen your other marketing efforts.

Building a Strong Brand Identity

A strong brand identity is the foundation of any successful marketing strategy. This is as important for internal marketing as it is for external marketing. As the CMO of your dental practice, it is imperative for you to ensure that your brand is consistently represented across all touchpoints, including the office environment, staff interactions, and marketing materials. When working on creating your internal marketing strategy and putting together systems for your different tactics, make sure that everything is "on brand." You can do this by asking the simple question "What would my avatar want?" and go from there. Your marketing company should be helping you create a brand identity as well—if they haven't addressed that, it might be time to find a new one. We'll talk more about how to do that in the external marketing section.

Enhancing Patient Experience

The most effective way to market a dental practice internally is to provide an exceptional patient experience. If this is the only thing you learn from this chapter —maybe even this book— it will change the trajectory of your practice. Provide unexpected levels of personalized care for each and every patient, and your practice will grow. This involves creating a welcoming and comfortable atmosphere, offering personalized care, and ensuring patients feel valued and heard. You can achieve this through the following actions:

- Training your staff to provide excellent customer service
- Giving a practice tour to new patients
- Implementing patient feedback systems to identify areas for improvement (Example: sending each patient a survey after their appointment, asking for ways to improve their experience)
- Offering amenities such as complimentary beverages, Wi-Fi, and entertainment options in the waiting area and noise-canceling headphones in treatment rooms
- Ensuring timely and efficient appointment scheduling
- Providing educational resources to help patients understand their treatment options and make informed decisions (without getting too deep into the specifics, which can induce fear!)
- Offering flexible payment plans or financing options to accommodate patients' financial needs—there's no better way to increase case acceptance than to increase affordability
- Implementing advanced technology and equipment to improve the quality of care and reduce treatment times

TIP: Don't get too specific when explaining treatment options to patients! Your patient doesn't need to know that you're going to be drilling ten millimeters into their bone—for most people, that's terrifying. They just need to know the basics: why this treatment is necessary, what level of pain they can expect, and confirmation that you know what you're doing. Providing too much detail can often induce fear, causing patients to postpone or avoid future treatment.

Every monthly team meeting we have a line item for Five-Star Experience, and everyone is responsible for looking for opportunities to either add or remove something from the patient experience that will increase enjoyment or decrease pain points. Including the team in this process has been instrumental in creating their buy-in to provide great service and has opened up many small ideas that have helped improve what we offer our patients. One small idea that came from this exercise is offering a hot towel after any dental procedure. It's a small, unexpected gesture that patients really appreciate.

Another element of improving patient experience is the office tour. At every new patient's comprehensive appointment, our patient concierge will give a practice tour. This tour is a fundamental part of our internal marketing process. Our patient concierge (a.k.a. receptionist) will first offer a comfort item like coffee or water and prepare it for the patient. (We have a Nespresso machine that can do all sorts of coffee drinks—it's awesome.) The tour begins first by showing the patient our Giving Wall, which is where we showcase our philanthropic efforts and invite the patient to join us in giving back to the community. (Usually this is something simple, like asking them if they want to contribute to a food drive or learn more about the charities we work with. We're certainly not asking them to write a check!) The tour includes discussing our technology and the benefit to the patient. An example is showing our CAD/

CAM mills to the patient and letting them know we can do most of their dental work in one visit, which will save them time, avoid temporaries, and improve the quality of work because the dentist is the one making the crown. We have specific patient benefits for each feature of our practice, from our open-bay sterilization center with tip-out bins to our CBCT. The "wow" factor here goes a long way in teaching them about our differentiating factors and helps them better share with their friends and family how we're different and better.

Leveraging Patient Testimonials and Reviews

When your team creates an unexpected positive experience for your patients, they'll want to tell people about it. (The same goes for a negative experience!) Positive patient testimonials and reviews are powerful tools for internal marketing. Encouraging satisfied patients to share their experiences can help build trust and credibility for the practice. You can do this in your practice in several ways:

- Request reviews from happy patients and feature them on the practice's website and social media channels. It's considered best practice to have the last team member of the visit say, "Tell me how your appointment went today." If it was a positive experience, your team member will request a review personally for whomever the patient saw: "I know your hygienist would love to hear about your great experience today. I'm going to send you a text this evening with a Google Review link. Would you mind giving a five-star review?"
- Display positive reviews in the office on bulletin boards or digital screens as well as sharing them with your team during huddles.

- Invite patients to record video testimonials. Everyone has evangelist patients—the ones that love you and tell everyone about your practice. These are the patients you invite to generate video testimonials to share on your practice's YouTube channel, website, and social media. Social proof is one of the most powerful tools in developing trust among your audience.

Implementing Referral Programs

Referral programs incentivize current patients to refer friends and family to the practice. These programs can be highly effective in attracting new patients and fostering loyalty among existing ones. Below are some suggestions on increasing referrals.

One tactic to increase patient referrals is to offer rewards such as discounts on future services, gift cards, or entry into a prize draw for patients who refer new clients. Promote the referral program through email newsletters, social media, and in-office signage. To leverage the referral program, you can do live monthly videos and share pictures on social media of the patient receiving their prize. Other best practices for implementing an internal referral program include the following:

- Tracking referrals to measure the program's success and making adjustments as needed
- Sending personalized, handwritten thank-you cards to anyone who refers a new patient
- Creating an incentivized referral program that's easy to understand and participate in
- Providing patients with referral cards or digital referral links to share with their friends and family
- Recognizing and rewarding patients who consistently refer new clients, such as featuring them in a Patient of the Month program

Engaging with Patients through Digital Channels

Social media has—for better or worse—become a way of life. I wouldn't say it's mandatory for your practice, but it's highly recommended. I have clients who use social media consistently with great results. I also have clients who have no social media presence and are doing just fine. To maximize all your internal marketing efforts, I highly suggest you or a team member actively engage in a social media campaign. In today's digital age, maintaining an active online presence is essential for marketing.

Social media applies to both internal and external marketing. It can, of course, be used to reach new patients through advertising and organic posts—something we'll cover in depth in the external marketing section of this chapter. But if you're only thinking about it in terms of acquiring new patients, you're missing out on some key benefits. Social media can also be used to engage with your current patients and keep them coming back to your practice.

Ideally, you'll want to think about how this applies to all your digital channels, such as your newsletter, blog, website, YouTube channel, and whatever other options you have at your disposal. Use these channels to engage with patients and keep them informed about the latest news, promotions, and services. This can be achieved by the following:

- Regularly updating your practice's website with relevant content, such as blog posts, service descriptions, and staff bios
- Sending email newsletters to keep patients informed about upcoming events, special offers, and dental health tips
- Engaging with patients on social media platforms like Facebook, Instagram, X, or TikTok by sharing informative posts and responding to comments (Consider posting about dentistry news, practice updates, fun non-dental-related stuff, and running contests or giveaways.)

> **TIP:** Remember, you're the CMO of your practice. While you should understand these tactics, that doesn't mean you'll be the one doing them. Everything I've just listed can (and ideally should) be outsourced to your marketing company or people on your team. If you're looking to save money and have the time, you can always do it yourself—but the goal should be to quickly remove yourself from this type of work.

Patient Education and Goal Setting

It's all too common to get stuck in a rut with our current patients. Joe and Sally have been coming at 10:00 a.m. on a Tuesday every six months for the last five years. Inevitably, the interaction can get a little stale:

> "How's the house coming along?"
>
> "Did your boy graduate yet?"
>
> "Any fun trips planned?"
>
> "Any concerns you'd like me to address in the eighteen seconds I have left for this exam?"
>
> "Everything looks stable—have a great [insert next holiday here]!"

This is a missed opportunity. Every year when I review the X-rays of a patient, I say some iteration of, "Hey, Joe, I wanted to check with you to see what goals you have for your oral health. Have you thought about making any changes to your smile?" I may also add a concern that I have for the patient's long-term oral health: "As we discussed previously, there's a lot of lower crowding with some excessive wear—have you thought about straightening those out so they can be as healthy as possible for as long as possible?" Simple questions with simple observations open up great conversations.

Since implementing this system with my patients, I've been able to help many patients improve their oral health and their confidence in their smile. When you implement this system and these easy questions, you'll be able to start doing more dentistry that people *want* rather than just telling them what they *need*. From a business perspective, this is key in creating a higher patient value. And when Joe shows off his new veneers at the golf course, it will increase patient referrals.

Don't overlook the dentistry that's already sitting in your chair, and don't be afraid to talk about it. Your patients come to you because they trust and like you. If you don't tell them what services are available to them, they might find someone else who they think does. I remember the terrible feeling when my patient came to an appointment with Invisalign from another local dentist. That was a failure on my part to educate and goal set with my patient.

In no way is this list exhaustive of all the tactics that can be employed for internal marketing, but these are the methods I recommend starting with. My suggestion is to introduce one new internal marketing tactic per quarter. Use the define, refine, and implement framework to work with your team on creating a new or improved internal marketing program.

The key is consistent implementation. This will result in transformative new patient growth and opportunities for your current patients to accept all your different treatment options. Internal marketing efforts are vital for the growth and success of your dental practice. By building a strong brand identity, enhancing patient experience, leveraging testimonials and reviews, implementing referral programs, and engaging with patients through digital channels, your dental practice can create a loyal patient base and attract new clients. These strategies not only help in promoting your practice but will also help your current patients have the best possible dental outcomes.

External Marketing: Fundamentals and Tactics

The goal of external marketing is to attract new patients who aren't associated with your practice or current patients. So at a high level, external marketing tactics include all the ways in which people who are not your current patients interact with you and your brand. The most common way this happens is through paid advertising, which comes in four main forms: print, digital, mass media, and something called ground marketing. We'll cover each of these advertising media so you have an idea of how to strategize what's right for your practice and communicate effectively with your marketing company.

Once again, I highly suggest you don't try to implement advertising on your own or through your brother's wife's cousin who "does marketing on the side." After helping develop the marketing strategy for hundreds of dental practices, I have seen what works and what doesn't—and your brother's wife's cousin doesn't work. The stakes and the costs are too high to risk the success of your practice to save a few bucks—it will cost you way more in the long run. Remember, external marketing is an investment, not a cost to be managed.

I'm hesitant to recommend one or even a few specific marketing companies because I can't necessarily guarantee the quality of a company over the long term. This is also something you'll need to be constantly evaluating. Just because you've worked with the same marketing company for a long time doesn't necessarily mean they're the best fit for you. You should always be evaluating their performance and considering your options.

So with that in mind, I've created the following worksheet to help you find a marketing company that works for you.

MARKETING COMPANY EVALUATION WORKSHEET

This worksheet is designed to help you evaluate potential dental marketing companies. Complete one for each company you're considering and compare results.

Company Information

Company Name: _____
Contact Person: _____
Date Evaluated: _____

Essential Criteria Checklist

Score each criterion as Yes (✓) or No (✗)

Dental Industry Focus

- Specializes in dental marketing
- Has experience with practices similar to yours
- Understands dental-specific regulations and compliance

Analytics and Tracking

- Provides access to Google Analytics
- Offers integration with your practice management software
- Can track marketing spend ROI
- Shows clear connection between marketing and new patient acquisition

Website and Content Ownership

- You maintain full ownership of website
- You have direct access to website backend
- Content is transferable if you change providers
- No proprietary/locked content systems

Contract Terms

- No long-term contract requirements
- Clear cancellation terms
- Transparent pricing structure
- Flexible service options

Proven Results

- Can provide case studies/examples
- Has references from similar practices
- Can show results from practices in comparable markets
- Presents clear metrics and KPIs

Questions to Ask

- What specific results have you achieved for practices similar to mine in terms of new patient acquisition?
- How do you track and report ROI?
- What is your typical timeframe for seeing results?
- How do you tailor marketing strategies for different dental practices?
- What happens to my website/content if we end our relationship?

Content and Brand Alignment

Rate each aspect 1-5 (1=Poor, 5=Excellent)

Quality of sample content: ___
Visual design: ___
Brand voice: ___
Target audience alignment: ___
Local market understanding: ___

Final Assessment

Total Checkmarks: ___/15
Content Rating Average: ___/5

Next Steps

☐ Proceed   ☐ Need More Information   ☐ Do Not Proceed

Keep in mind that your role as the CMO is to hold your marketing company accountable to the results they're promising you. You need to be able to analyze what they're doing and ask the right questions to ensure they're doing what they say they're doing. You also need to understand enough about marketing to make sure their approach is sound. My goal for this portion of the book is to help you develop a baseline level of understanding that will allow you to do exactly that. You don't need to be able to implement everything yourself or understand all the nitty-gritty details; you just need to know enough to effectively work with your marketing company.

To start, there are three marketing fundamentals you need to be aware of as the CMO of your practice: authenticity, quality, and reach. These alone will be instrumental in your marketing efforts.

Fundamental #1: Authenticity

The first fundamental is that your advertising must be a true representation of you, your brand, and your services. Don't allow an agency or consultant to recommend a tactic that strays from authenticity. Dentistry is a specifically personal profession that's built on trust. If your advertising doesn't reflect the essence of your practice, your values, and your services, it can make developing trust much more difficult. When your marketing company has a suggestion that goes against your authenticity, it's an opportunity to help them better understand who you are and how you operate. This will improve the quality of their suggestions moving forward.

At Thrive Family Dental, we don't offer promotions, discounts, sales, or other advertising tactics around pricing for our services other than a new patient special (more on this later). We've defined our avatar, and I'm continually refining our messaging to increase the quality of our patients. My office doesn't have "in-office advertising" of posters, pamphlets, or brochures to distract patients from our curated experience. Not offering discounted services helps our patients value the work we do and sets an expectation that our fees are our fees. I've worked through this with my advertising company, and now we no longer have discussions on that particular tactic.

I'm in no way saying this specific advertising tactic is wrong. It can be effective in helping patients reach the right dentist. As I mentioned previously, "rational people respond to incentives," and discounts can be an effective way to increase sales. In my practice, that's an advertising tactic that doesn't reflect my brand, so I don't use it. The goal is to make tactical decisions with advertising that are authentic to you and your brand.

Fundamental #2: Quality

You can expect a potential patient to judge the quality of your work based on the quality of your marketing and advertising. In essence, quality attracts quality. When you create excellent and high-quality advertising, you are communicating to your patients what they can expect from you. If you have a great website and a beautiful office with the greatest technology, and then you shoot a video on a four-year-old cell phone with terrible lighting and it sounds like you're in a metal silo, then your potential patients likely won't even make it to the end. Now you've wasted your time, money, and opportunity. Critically analyze the quality of the advertising you're putting out and make sure it's reflective of you and your brand.

Fundamental #3: Reach

Another fundamental aspect of external marketing is something called *reach*. This is the number of potential patients that will be exposed to your advertising. More isn't necessarily better—it's just more. In today's day and age, reaching lots of people isn't difficult—the problem tends to be more around how to reach the right patients for your practice. There are two aspects of reach to keep in mind when developing an advertising strategy that will help you navigate that problem. The two guiding questions are "How wide?" and "To Whom?"

For instance, the "How wide?" question helps you determine where to advertise. It doesn't make sense to spend a lot of money on a postcard mailer campaign that will reach a twenty-mile radius around your practice when you live in a suburban region. Most people's lives are lived in a three to five-mile radius in the suburbs, and they pick their service providers based on that circle. Sure, you may have patients who come and see you from farther away. We wear the "My patients drive from two hours away to see me" badge of honor proudly, but it isn't because they got a postcard—and I don't suggest spending the money to learn that lesson on your own. Target your advertising based on the buying habits of your market. The radius should increase as the dentistry of the population decreases. For instance, some patients in New York City might not even walk more than three or four blocks to go to the dentist. But in a rural setting it might be the entire county.

The question "To whom?" helps with targeting. For your marketing to be effective, you want to make sure the right people are seeing your messaging. If you're a general dentist that wants to see the whole family, it would make sense to advertise specifically to that demographic: women aged thirty to forty-five years old, middle-class income, and starter- to mid-sized homes. Conversely, if you're looking for esthetically driven patients who want facial esthetics and cosmetic dentistry, your demographic would look more like this: forty-six to sixty-five years old, middle- to high-income, living in high-net-worth neighborhoods. If you're not entirely sure how to handle this, you should be able to work with your marketing company to come up with a demographic that makes sense based on your avatar.

As you're developing your external marketing strategy, there's another guiding question I'd like to add: "How does this advertising campaign put patients in my chair?" Each ad should have a direct call to action and anticipated response. A call to action or CTA is marketing-speak for what you want the person to do after seeing the advertisement. For instance, if you're creating a social media advertisement, there should be a CTA button at the bottom that says something like, "Click here to schedule." This type of advertising—where someone can take action right away—is called direct-response marketing, and it's one of the best ways for any small- to medium-size business to market because it encourages action right away and lets you gauge how well people are responding to your advertising. Large corporations like Pepsi and Coke can afford to advertise everywhere solely for branding purposes, but you are not them. All ads need to direct people down the path toward making an appointment, not just tell them about you or your brand.

When you use these fundamentals and proper targeting, your advertising dollars will be spent more efficiently. It's not uncommon to use the "see what sticks" mentality for advertising. Don't do it. This is a quick way to become disillusioned with the benefit of external marketing. External marketing is effective when done properly. If you set a budget, track your results, and calculate the ROI of each campaign using the method we covered in chapter 8, and you'll be able to home in on what works and what doesn't—and your marketing will be successful.

Now that we've brushed the surface of external marketing, let's dive into the specific tactics.

Digital Advertising

Digital advertising stands out as the most effective strategy for general dentists in today's market. By concentrating on the two primary platforms—Google and Meta—you can maximize the impact of your marketing budget. Focusing your efforts on these channels will likely yield the best results for attracting new patients and growing your practice.

Google is very specific in that you'll be using it almost exclusively for advertising. Meta, on the other hand, is a social media platform that also has advertising. While I do recommend using it for advertising, I also recommend putting time into creating a great social media presence for your practice. That means your practice's social media account should ideally be up-to-date, well-branded, and posting high-quality content on a regular basis. We'll talk about how all that works when we get into organic and paid social media, but for now, let's discuss the digital advertising giant that is Google.

Google

For Google, our focus will be on Google Ads, which is one of their primary advertising services. There are a number of more nuanced ways to use Google for advertising, but Google Ads is the best place to start. It's important to quickly differentiate between SEO and Google Ads, which are sometimes used interchangeably but are very different strategies.

- **SEO** is a long-term tactic that involves maximizing the efficiency of your website, creating website content that's relevant to your readers, and developing a "trust factor" with Google based on its current algorithm rules to place your website at the top of the search results without having to give Google money. SEO is a long game. It's a very complicated tactic and not one we will dive into in this book, but it can be effective at increasing new patient flow over the long-term.

- **Google Ads** is a tactic used to place an advertisement for your dental office at the top of the search results when specific key words such as "best dentist near me" are searched in Google. You can choose the exact keyword(s) you'd like your advertisements to appear under, and you pay Google each time your advertisement is shown. Unlike SEO, Google Ads can start generating results almost immediately.

Because of the ever-evolving arena of digital marketing and the growth of Google competitors, the way you engage in your digital advertising is going to vary over time, and the specific tactics may have changed by the time you get to this chapter. For this reason, we're going to cover the high-level methodologies you need to know and how to hold your advertising company accountable for results.

The major benefit of Google Ads is the concept of a ready buyer. Someone is looking for a specific service, searches for that service or provider, and Google puts an organized list in front of them. This person is *actively looking for a dentist* and your name pops up toward the top of the list. It doesn't get much easier from an advertising position. This is in contrast to a billboard, for example. A billboard is a picture with a limited message put in front of a distracted driver with the hope that one day, when they need a dentist, they'll remember your name because they saw it on a billboard two months ago.

When creating an ad campaign for Google Ads, make sure that you're only paying for ads for keywords that reflect the dentistry you want to do. When I started with my marketing company, we had a Google Ads campaign for dentures. I make dentures, so they thought it would be a good opportunity to grow the business and created a denture keyword campaign. I then had to inform them that just because I make dentures doesn't mean I enjoy it or want to do more of it! Another example is pediatrics. I see kids, but I don't want to see a lot of them, so I instructed my marketing company to not include keywords for pediatrics. This is why you need to be involved in your marketing. You don't want to pay for advertising for procedures you don't want to do—but your marketing company won't have that knowledge unless you communicate it to them.

When deciding on different Google Ads campaigns for specific procedures, it's important to remember that specificity and competition will change the cost. Google Ads is a bidding system, which means the more competitive your market and the more specific the procedure, the higher the bid will need to be before it's seen by a potential patient. If you're interested in placing more implants or doing more clear aligner therapy, and you use Google Ads to drive those patients into your practice, you can expect to pay more in your ad spend. Those procedures are specific, limited, and highly competitive, so the advertising costs to acquire those will be higher. In some markets, those can be two or three times more expensive when compared to a general campaign such as "dentist near me."

In reality, Google Ads is even more complicated than I'm making it out to be here. What's most important is that you understand these high-level fundamentals and that you're working with a marketing company that has specific expertise with Google Ads. There are people who build their entire careers around this, and your marketing company should have those people on their staff.

> **TIP:** Be efficient with your time and energy! I don't advise clients to learn how to run advertising campaigns. That's someone else's specialty. We are dentists, and our nonclinical time should be spent learning how to improve our skills in dentistry, communication, and leadership. Focus on the things that only you can do and outsource the rest.

Another important element of digital advertising is something called A/B testing. In short, there should always be two competing advertising campaigns happening simultaneously. It might sound counterintuitive to compete against yourself, but the idea is that one of the campaigns will outperform the other, showing you what's working. The advertising team will then use that knowledge to tweak the losing option until it becomes the better-performing ad. Then they tweak the new loser, and so on. This prevents your digital advertising from becoming stagnant and allows for maximum efficiency. Make sure your marketing company has a program in place for this—otherwise your ad budget may not be as effective as possible.

Organic Social Media

When it comes to social media marketing, there are endless approaches. For our purposes, we're going to focus on the biggest player in the room: Meta. This is where the majority of your potential patients will be. I know there's TikTok and Snapchat and LinkedIn and X and maybe three new ones by the time you're reading this. From a marketing and advertising perspective, Meta will cover the vast majority of needs for a dental practice marketing campaign.

Within social media marketing, the two terms to define are *organic* and *paid. Organic social media marketing* is using the available free features of posting self-made content to a platform in hopes of reaching potential patients. *Paid social media advertising* is when you pay to put your message in front of a specific, preselected audience. Both have specific benefits and drawbacks.

Having an organic presence on social media is a positive for your practice. It's not required, but it will help you acquire new patients. I recall having a conversation with my wife about where we should go out to eat, and I suggested a restaurant she hadn't heard of. She immediately grabbed her phone and searched for the restaurant on Instagram to "social media stalk" them. She wanted to see the atmosphere, the food, the team, and ultimately learn the "personality" of the establishment. Using social media as a means to vet a restaurant is well-established, and the same thing is happening to your dental practice.

In my office, we'll routinely hear patients say things like, "I knew you were the practice for me because I saw your Instagram post that said . . ." For a long time, people were mostly mentioning our website and Google reviews, but now we're hearing about our social media presence more and more. It's become a tool for the consumer to make a better-informed decision of where they want to put their trust. Picking a dentist is a scary decision for patients, and the more we can help them, the better—a vibrant and approachable social media presence goes a long way.

When creating your organic social media presence, there are four main categories of posts to think about: authentic posts, authority posts, fun posts, and potpourri posts.

Authentic Posts

Think of these as the non-doctor and non-dental posts about the people in your practice, including you. Who are you? What do you do for fun? How do you relate to the world? The more authentic you are, the more people can get to know you, and the more trust you'll be able to build. Remember that you want to attract like-minded people who you have things in common with, so this is one strong way for those people to find you.

One of the doctors I coach *loves* to dance! She'll routinely post a video of her sharing gratitude and doing a dance to a song she loves. Other times, she'll share a struggle she's currently wrestling with and dance to make herself feel better. It's a true reflection of who she is. It's authentic and it's effective at bringing her patients that love to share in her joy. Be authentically you, and it will build trust and a competitive advantage over dentists that aren't doing the same.

A quick disclaimer: The nature of these posts can make some doctors or team members a bit uncomfortable. Only share what you want about what you want and don't feel like you need to share everything. You get to set the boundaries here. It's your practice, so you get to do what you want! Just don't try to be someone you're not.

Authority Posts

These posts are designed to showcase the quality of your work and your dental knowledge—in other words, you're showing potential patients that you are in fact a great dentist. That said, please—for the love of hematopoiesis—*do not post bloody pictures!* Your audience is a mother of three or a retired New Englander—not other dentists! Post a nice before-and-after of ten veneers or a crumbling amalgam turned into a conservative Emax onlay. Patients don't want to see how the sausage is made. Posting Q&A videos of common questions is also an easy way to show your knowledge and approachability. The key here is to use common words and lay terms. (Avoid words like *hematopoiesis*.)

Fun Posts

Hopefully this is self-explanatory. Be sure to spend some time creating and sharing posts that are just plain fun! This could be your team participating a new viral trend or learning the current dance move. There are endless ways to engage in the fun category, and the best way to find them is to ask your team. When creating this type of post, it's important that you don't do things only other dentists or dental teams would find funny. "Let's laugh about patients being afraid of the needle! Hahaha!" Absolutely not. Don't make fun of your audience—what we find funny as professionals inside the industry is often the exact thing that a potential patient might fear or feel judged by.

As I write this, there's a trend in dental social media mentioning palatal petechiae and saying, "We know." It may get a chuckle from other dental providers, but a potential patient who's researching your office may either be offended by it or afraid of feeling embarrassed when they walk into your practice. The purpose of fun posts is to show your office has a positive work environment and to create an approachable vibe. So think from the perspective of what your avatar—not other dental providers—would want to see before posting these videos.

Potpourri Posts

These are ad-hoc posts based on something that's currently happening inside or outside of your practice. So it could be a post of your team talking like pirates for "speak like a pirate day," or it might be an announcement that you're sponsoring a 5k run for charity. Maybe a patient of yours is opening a new restaurant and you'd like to give them a shout-out. Go for it! These types of posts do a great job of balancing out your social media feed and helping you reach a larger audience.

One thing to mention before we talk about the paid advertising part of social media is paid organic. Paid organic is paying for someone to post organic content on your behalf. It's rarely worth it. In most cases, the process starts out well, and they post pictures and video content that you already have on-hand. They might come to the office once or twice to get more content and post that too. Then each party gets too busy, and the posts become more and more stale, don't reflect the doctor or team authentically, and eventually spiral into canned content from stock photography until all life is sucked out of the page. I know this from personal experience, from my clients' experience, and from researching other brands. It's immediately obvious when you see a brand being managed by an outside third party.

One of the most effective strategies for creating a vibrant organic social media presence is to delegate management of your account to someone on your team. Discover who's interested in social media and willing to take on this responsibility, then provide them with the tools and resources to learn about social media strategies and create a system around it. *Define, refine, and implement* an organic social media role in your office and include everyone. The more involved your team is, the better the results will be. Remember to have fun!

Before we move on to the paid advertising portion of social media, it's important to mention another benefit of having great organic content. A frequently updated, high-quality, engaging social media presence will drastically increase the effectiveness of your paid advertising. If you pay Meta to put your message in front of potential patients who click on your ad only to see a social media page filled with stock photos and generic descriptions, you're not going to convert many of those people into new patients. The same could be said for other forms of advertising too—many people who hear your ad on the radio or see you on television will first check your social media accounts to learn more about you. That's just the world we live in nowadays. As such, I recommend posting across your social channels at least once per week—but ideally more.

Paid Social Media

So, now that we've covered the basics on organic social media strategy, let's jump into paid social media—in other words, advertising. This is where your dollars can be put to incredible use with great ROI, and also where you can light your Benjamins on fire and wave them in the air (which isn't a great viral video idea, by the way). There's a ton of power in social media advertising, so let's dive in.

Advertising on social media is incredibly powerful because of its specificity. Google advertising allows specificity for what people are looking for in the search bar, whereas Meta allows you to put yourself directly in front of the specific demographic you're looking to attract. It's really quite incredible. If you want to get your ad in front of a woman in her thirties who was recently engaged and lives within five miles of your office, who is also a Republican and likes to run—you can do that. Seriously, you can be that specific. You can also do things like retargeting people who have visited your website or people who have viewed other dentists in your area.

The power in that type of specificity allows you, as an advertiser, to create ad campaigns that are tailored to a small group of people. Because they're extremely specific to that individual audience, they tend to be far more effective than more traditional forms of advertising. For instance, with the newly-engaged audience, you could offer a consultation for a pre-wedding esthetic evaluation.

And while you might think this specificity comes at a cost, it shockingly doesn't. For the amount of exposure you can buy and the number of impressions you can get (how many people see your ad), advertising through Meta is actually very affordable. Some doctors see significant results with budgets in the hundreds instead of thousands of dollars. The relatively low cost allows you to take more risks—you can get creative with your posts, and if they don't land, it's not a huge cost to pivot to a new campaign. This is where the "art" of advertising comes in. On the flip side, if they do land, you can get some incredible results.

A few other benefits of advertising on Meta are the interactive nature of the ads and the ability to retarget. One ad that did well for me a few years ago was a "use it or lose it" ad that we ran in Q4. We had a simple script and recorded a video of each one of my team members lifting weights with bright-pink dumbbells. It wasn't some massive production, but we were smiling and having fun. We posted this ad to our specific demographic with a small budget behind it—and it got a *ton* of interaction. The comments ranged from joking about how strong I must be to lift eight-pound weights to: "If they have this much fun, I want them to be my dentist." It was also reshared several times, and the ad took on a bit of a life of its own. We then retargeted the people who'd interacted with that ad and continued to make sure they were included in future ad demographics.

When working on an ad for Meta, the more interaction (likes, comments, or shares) it gets, the less expensive the ad becomes over time. Meta wants to increase engaging content to its users.

If your ad is engaging, they charge less per impression. The exact opposite is true as well. If your post is devoid of all life, it will be more expensive to show to your target market. That's why, once again, it pays to be authentic and approachable on social media.

Meta ads can be very difficult to figure out, so I don't recommend using your extremely valuable time learning how to advertise. Most marketing companies will charge a modest fee of $500 to $1,000 to run these campaigns and run them more effectively than you would. Remember from the KPI section that you should be collecting $1,000 an hour or more. I'd guess it would take at least $5,000 worth of your time to learn how to set up and manage a campaign—one that will surely generate worse results than if you hired a specialist to do it. (See: waving fiery Benjamins in the air.)

When you're strategizing an ad campaign with your marketing company, you need to build your ads backward. Use the DRI framework. Define what you want the result to be first. For instance: "I want to attract new patients that are interested in esthetic rehabs." Once you know the result you want, you can refine it by defining the demographic and determining messaging that will reach them. This might be a middle-aged to newly-retired female with moderate to high income who owns her home and is interested in high fashion and cosmetics. Do some research into the types of advertisements that might be targeting that demographic and then brainstorm how you want to communicate to that group. Then create that ad and send it. Adjust the demographic and the ad spend, then try to create a second ad that's a bit different and test it against the first.

Social media advertising is a constantly-moving target that is ever-evolving with changes in technology, trends, and culture. That means what worked last year might not work this year. The key to successful use of social media is to have a robust organic presence that communicates the "who we are" tied to poignant, emotion-driven advertisements that lead people to take action and schedule an appointment. When you have that, and it's targeting the right people in the right place, then you'll have a successful social media marketing strategy.

Community Engagement

Don't make the mistake of thinking advertising is your only option for external marketing. Community engagement—specifically, getting out and meeting people—can be one of the most powerful ways to build your practice. (When done right, that is.)

Now, if you're picturing yourself sitting behind a table at an expo, waiting for people to grab your business card and hoping they might schedule an appointment—that's exactly what you *don't* want to do. Real community engagement is about being active, creating memorable experiences, and having genuine interactions with potential patients. When you do that effectively, these events can have a huge impact on your practice.

Why is this so powerful? Because when you're engaging potential patients outside of your office, the walls break down. Dentists are often seen as intimidating or scary to patients. Picking a dentist is a tough decision that often leads to potential patients not making a decision at all. Using community-engagement marketing meets patients where they are, breaks down the walls between patient and doctor, creates a warm relationship, and builds trust outside the operatory. It reduces the challenges to picking a dentist. When these patients come to your office, they're more likely to commit to treatment sooner and refer friends and family. Compare that to a patient coming into your office from a quick "dentist near me" search and a cursory review of your website. There's a lot more work to do to build trust with that patient compared to, for example, the one you met at a volunteer event painting over graffiti.

When we talk about community engagement, I think of it as falling into one of four buckets:

1. **Local Events**
2. **Collaborations**
3. **Community Outreach**
4. **Public Relations**
5. **Networking**

A quick brainstorming session (with or without your team) can help you identify which methods you'd like to employ—although ideally, it would be a combination of all four. I suggest thinking of these efforts like you would any other marketing campaign. *Define* what you're going to do, *refine* it by putting a strategy in place, and *implement* it. You can only go to so many events or spend so much time networking—and unfortunately, it can be difficult to track the ROI of some of these efforts—so you'll want to think carefully about which methods are most aligned with your business and your goals.

Your vision, mission, and core values can also be helpful here. These can (and should!) inform you on which opportunities make the most sense for your business. If the event, person, or organization is aligned with your vision, mission, and core values, that's a great sign. If not, you might want to pass. Let's take a closer look at each.

Local Events

You can sponsor or participate in community fairs, school events, health expos, and farmers' markets to build visibility and rapport. These can be a lot of fun! There are a few key factors for success at these types of events.

The first thing to do is have a table banner and a vertical stand-alone banner made with your logo and contact information. Move the table to the back or side of the booth so there's no barrier between you and your potential patients. And get rid of the chairs! You won't be needing them. Be creative with your booth's theme, such as creating a game, a challenge, or an interactive exhibit that intrigues people.

One of our most successful events was a family expo. Our interactive game was for kids to teach their parents "how to floss" (this is a dance, for those of you who are even more out of the loop than I am). We gave away succulent plants with our logo on them when the parents successfully did the dance. These were real plants, by the way—not some cheap piece of plastic swag that would've been thrown away long before they got to their car. We had a line of people waiting to try because we were having fun, we were standing up and engaging the attendees, and we had great, high-quality swag. Compare this to your typical booth with two people sitting behind a table, staring at their phones with a bowl of candy and some pens with their logo on it.

Another way to improve your "return" on these events is to enter people into a giveaway in exchange for booking an appointment. Simply ask, "Do you want to schedule you and your family for an appointment?" and then point to your sign with an Amazon gift card (or whatever prize you choose) on it. "Anyone who schedules their family today will be entered into the drawing!" This is how to turn a good booth into a great booth! *Appointments* are always the goal.

Collaborations

Another great way to engage with your community is through partnerships with local businesses like gyms, salons, and schools. These collaborations can involve dental health seminars, exclusive discounts, or cross-promotions—and when done right, they're a win-win for everyone involved.

The key lesson I've learned is that instead of just offering your standard promotions, frame them as *coming from your partner.* For example, let's say you already offer free whitening or an electric toothbrush as part of your new patient special. You could work with a local gym where they "offer" this promotion to their clients. They might post on social media something like, "Because oral health is part of total health, we've partnered with [your practice] to offer our members a free electric toothbrush!"

The beauty of this approach is that it costs you nothing extra—you're just repackaging a promotion you already have. The gym gets to support a local business and show they care about their members' total health, while you get access to an entirely new audience. The key to a great collaboration is making it a win-win for both parties. If you go into it with the mindset of "What can I get out of this?" you're thinking about it wrong. Instead, flip your thinking to

"What value can I provide for them and their audience?" People will be much more receptive to your ask, and they'll naturally want to reciprocate.

Community Outreach

If the idea of helping people while growing your practice intrigues you, then you should really be looking into community outreach opportunities. Consider offering free dental checkups or presentations at local schools, community centers, and nursing homes. The key here is consistency. A one-off visit to a community center might feel good, but it won't move the needle for your practice—or your community! However, if you commit to monthly visits over the course of a year, you'll build a valuable pool of potential patients while making a meaningful difference.

Public Relations

Local publications are always hungry for content, especially from experts in their field. By writing articles about dental health for local newspapers, blogs, and neighborhood magazines, you can position yourself as the go-to dental expert in your area. This strategy can be very effective.

Getting started is simple. Look for journalists who have written articles on subjects you want to talk about. If it's the importance of oral cancer screenings at every visit, then search for journalists who have written about cancer. Once you have that list, simply email them to ask if they'd like to collaborate on an article relating to cancer and dentistry. If you do this once, to one journalist, and never follow up, it won't work. This is an effort that has the potential for profound impact for your business, but it can take months of consistent effort. I have a very specific process I use for this—if you're interested in learning more about it, that's something we can cover through one-on-one coaching or in my mastermind.

Networking

When it comes to networking, I give all my clients the same advice: pick one organization—and only one—to join. Try to find an organization that meets frequently and is aligned with your vision, mission, and core values. And this might sound obvious, but make sure you can actually attend their meetings! There were many groups I wanted to join, but 9:00 a.m. on a Tuesday twice per month just wasn't feasible.

Once you've selected your organization, it's vital that you *go to their events*! Show up and be intentional. Keep your phone in your pocket, embrace the awkwardness, and talk to people you don't know. I know it's uncomfortable, but there's no magic wand to this—you've just got to dive in. One thing that might help is to remember that a majority of the people there are just like you: nervous in big groups and hoping to find someone to talk to. That means when you go talk to someone, you're doing them a favor, and they'll be thankful for it. The other thing to remember is that as a doctor, there's already a level of respect and esteem that they offer you immediately. It's rare that the doctor shows up to these events personally—they'll often send a team member in their place. When you show up in person, it makes a much greater impact.

Creating rapport with members of your community opens up a large web of opportunities and referrals. Our practice has received countless referrals from people who have never stepped foot in our building. That's the power of networking. Business leaders, community leaders, and public officials all attend these events, and when you show up consistently and engage meaningfully, your network naturally expands. My involvement with my local Chamber of Commerce has led to me being named one of the "Forty Under Forty Most Influential People," being selected for a community service program called Leadership Wilmington, and even being voted Entrepreneur of the Year—as a dentist!

Like everything else we've covered in this book, your community engagement efforts should follow the *define*, *refine*, and *implement* framework. Start by defining which events you want to participate in and what specific outcomes you're hoping to achieve. Then refine your strategy by working with your marketing company and team to create engaging experiences that lead to appointments. Finally, implement a long-term plan to maintain these efforts.

Remember, this isn't a "one-and-done" strategy. Community engagement is an ongoing commitment to meeting people outside your office to build relationships, build trust, and build brand awareness.

Embracing Your Role as CMO

As the chief marketing officer of your dental practice, you hold the reins of your marketing and advertising strategy. I know this can seem like a daunting task, and one that you're probably not terribly interested in. But I hope I've made it clear that you don't need to know every nitty-gritty aspect of marketing to successfully market your practice. If you do happen to know the difference between CPM, CPC, CPM, CPP, and CRO (just a short list of the more than fifteen marketing acronyms starting with *C*)—great. If not, I hope this chapter has at least equipped you with enough knowledge to say, "WTF?" to your marketing company—you know, "What's this fee?" (What? Did you think I was referring to something else?)

On a more serious note, your responsibility as a healthcare entrepreneur is to oversee and empower others to execute your vision effectively. As the CMO of your practice, you need to ensure that your marketing efforts are aligned with your brand values, attract the right patients, and foster a strong connection with your patient family. Think of it as putting together a puzzle: You don't have to carve the pieces yourself, but you do need to know what the final picture should look like. By embracing internal strategies like enhancing the patient experience, leveraging testimonials, and implementing referral programs alongside external strategies such as digital advertising, social media campaigns, and community engagement, you'll set your practice up for sustainable growth—and maybe even a few "wow!" moments.

The key is to delegate effectively while staying involved in high-level decision-making. Collaborate with marketing professionals and your team to define clear goals, refine approaches based on feedback and performance, and implement consistent, high-quality campaigns. Trust in the expertise of your marketing partners, but remember: You're the captain of this ship, not just a passenger along for the ride.

Marketing isn't just about getting patients through the door—it's about building lasting relationships, creating memorable experiences, and communicating the unique value of your care. And who doesn't want patients leaving their office talking about how their dentist is both a great dentist and a trusted friend? By adopting the mindset of a healthcare entrepreneur, you'll not only grow your practice, but also make sure it's the kind of place your patients brag about to their friends (and on their Facebook feed).

Define, Refine, Implement

Define: Identify your marketing goals and communicate them to your marketing company.

Refine: Plan and adjust your approaches based on feedback and performance.

Implement: Be active with consistent, high-quality campaigns! (And track your results!)

PHILANTHROPY

You've worked incredibly hard to get where you are today. You've overcome countless obstacles, hurdles, roadblocks, and any other synonyms for "setback" you'd like to include. You were able to achieve this because of your work ethic, intense focus, and innate talent, yes. But the reality is that there were also many people in your life who helped you with that lift. Now that you're in a place of great influence and income, you have an opportunity to be the person who lifts *others* up. You get to be the person who breaks down barriers to help others in their pursuit of a fulfilled life. You get to *give*.

If I were to define philanthropy, I'd say it's the act of giving to promote the welfare of others. In other words, using your money to help people with no expectation of a direct return on your investment. Now, I know what you're thinking: "But, Ben, how am I going to build a seven-figure practice if I'm giving all of my money away?"

Well, first of all, you won't be giving all of your money away. This also might not be something you're able to do until your business grows more. If you're struggling to make ends meet right now, then by all means, don't concern yourself with philanthropy. But the point of this chapter is to illustrate how philanthropy is more than just a noble endeavor; it's also a strategic investment in your practice, your team, and your community. By embracing giving, fostering a culture of generosity, finding personal and professional fulfillment, and building a stellar reputation, you create a legacy that extends far beyond the dental chair. So go ahead and let your philanthropic spirit shine—your community, your team, and your heart will thank you for it.

The Benefits of Philanthropy

In chapter 1, we talked about defining your vision—the impact you want to have, how you want to be remembered, the legacy you want to leave. We then spent nine chapters building the foundation for a highly profitable practice through leadership, management, and marketing. Now, we've reached the point where it all comes full circle: With a thriving practice, you have the capacity—both in terms of time and resources—to create that impact and build that legacy through philanthropy.

This is the moment when running a successful practice enables you to fulfill your original vision. The profitability and systems you've built give you the freedom to volunteer, donate, and make a meaningful difference in your community. This is what we've been working toward. To me, it's the ultimate end goal: to have a business that is so fulfilling and profitable that it enables you to give back to those in need and those who helped you along the way. When I first mentioned the DRI framework, I explained how you could think of it like the process for building your dream home. You'd first *define* your dream home, *refine* it by creating the blueprint, and *implement* it by building the house. Now, this is like opening the doors of your dream house and sharing it with the people, communities, and organizations you care about most.

When I first dove into philanthropy in my own practice, I didn't expect much to come from it. I looked at philanthropy as a donation—something that would make me feel good and help me give back to the community. But what I realized was that when you give back authentically, in ways that are aligned with your vision and values, it has many other benefits. It strengthens your brand, improves patient trust, and ultimately increases profitability, which enables even greater impact.

There are many tangible benefits that come from philanthropy as a business owner, so let's explore them.

Personal and Professional Fulfillment

As a dentist, you know the power of a bright smile. Philanthropy isn't just about writing checks; it's about creating a ripple effect of positivity that touches lives far beyond your practice walls. When you invest in your community, it's not just about oral health for one patient—it's about improving the lives of everyone around you. I know on a Thursday afternoon that a #30 DO composite on "micro-mouth Bob" can be an absolute drag. Having a significant and meaningful philanthropic effort helps you stay motivated beyond the dentistry you excel at.

Imagine being an engaged sponsor and volunteering with a local youth sports team, or organizing free dental checkups for underserved communities. These acts of kindness not only improve oral health, but also build bridges of trust and goodwill. Your patients see you not just as a dentist, but a pillar of the community. Your team sees someone who genuinely cares about more than just the bottom line.

Let's face it: Running a dental practice can be stressful. Between managing appointments, dealing with insurance, and ensuring top-notch patient care, it's easy to feel overwhelmed. Philanthropy offers a refreshing break from the hustle and bustle. It provides a sense of personal and professional fulfillment that goes beyond the confines of your practice. When you give back, you reconnect with the core reason you became a dentist: to help people. It's a reminder of the bigger picture and the impact you can make. Whether it's through mentoring young dental students, supporting dental missions abroad, or contributing to local health initiatives, philanthropy enriches your life in ways that money can't buy.

It's also worth considering that philanthropy isn't a solo act; it's a team sport. Remember, when you involve your staff in charitable activities, you create a culture of giving that boosts morale and job satisfaction. Picture your team volunteering at a local shelter, providing free dental care to those in need. The camaraderie and sense of purpose that come from these experiences are priceless. Your team members feel proud to be part of a practice that values giving back. It fosters a sense of belonging and loyalty, making them more engaged and motivated in their daily work. Plus, it's a fantastic way to break the monotony of the daily grind.

When you create opportunities to give to others, you hit every topic in THRIVE—those essential elements of job satisfaction: *triumph*, *happiness*, *relationships*, *involvement*, *vitality*, and *environment*. There's a sense of triumph and accomplishment in volunteering. Giving creates feelings of gratitude, which is one of the leading predictors of happiness. The time spent together bonding in service builds deeper relationships. Your team feels involved in something greater than themselves or even the dental practice where they work. These activities promote vitality by changing gears and getting everyone out of the office. And I can say from personal experience that the whole process is very enjoyable. It makes you feel good, it's fun, and everyone comes back to work feeling more energized, with a greater sense of purpose.

Don't believe me? I've got a story for you.

Recruitment

A couple years ago, I had an interesting opportunity to work with someone outside of the dental industry. A dental colleague of mine from Ideal Practices reached out to me about a business owner he'd met in Puerto Rico who could use my help with incorporating philanthropy into his business.

The business was Roof Maxx, a roofing company with over $300,000,000 in annual sales. The owner, Mike, had learned about the philanthropic work I'd done with dentists and was intrigued about doing something similar in his business. He'd grown Roof Maxx quickly and received numerous awards, but he wanted his company to stand for something more. He wanted to give back and create a bigger impact.

Over a six-month engagement, we took his company through the same in-depth process we use with dental practices to discover their authentic passion for philanthropy—much of which we'll cover in this chapter. His entire team of C-suite officers participated as we helped them craft their vision, mission, and core values to ensure any philanthropic partnership they created would be authentic and impactful.

Mike had a powerful personal experience that resonated deeply with his team. On a trip to Mexico, he befriended a young boy named Miguel who sold bracelets in the plaza. They'd see each other often, communicating through broken Spanish and English. One night, as Mike returned to his hotel, he was shocked to discover Miguel among a group of homeless children huddled on cardboard in a doorway. The hotel key weighed heavily in his hand as he thought about those without a place to call home.

This experience changed him forever, and it led Mike and his team to partner with the Dave Thomas Foundation for Adoption. Now, whenever Roof Maxx restores a roof, they help provide a forever home to a child in the foster care system. By 2030, they're projected to give close to half a million dollars to this cause, which will help 25,000 foster children find forever homes. Their mission isn't just to build better roofs—it's to improve the lives of foster children across the country.

Surprisingly (or maybe not so surprisingly given what we've already covered), this also had a significant impact on the company's hiring process. When I checked in after our engagement, they shared that recruitment had become both cheaper and easier. They were consistently attracting high-level, highly skilled employees for less money than their competitors were offering. Nearly all these recruits who passed on "better" opportunities said they did so because they wanted to work for a company that led with its values and allowed them to make a bigger impact in the world.

This shouldn't be surprising. When you create an authentic philanthropic partnership and incorporate it into your practice's identity, it becomes a powerful recruiting tool. Be sure to mention your philanthropic efforts in job descriptions and during your hiring process. Not only is this a considerable benefit to many prospective employees, but it will naturally attract people who are aligned with your vision, mission, and core values.

I've kept most of the examples in this book specific to dentists, but I wanted to share this one with you to illustrate how these are proven principles that work regardless of industry. If it can work for a nine-figure roofing company, it can work for your practice.

Reputation within Your Community

In the world of business, reputation is everything. For a dental practice, a good reputation can mean the difference between a full waiting room and an empty one. Philanthropy plays a crucial role in building and maintaining a positive image in your community. When people see your commitment to giving back, they associate your practice with trust, integrity, and compassion.

Word of mouth is a powerful tool, and nothing spreads faster than stories of generosity and kindness. Your philanthropic efforts become a talking point, attracting new patients who value a dentist who cares about more than just teeth. It's another win-win: You get to make a difference, and your practice thrives as a result.

What *Not* to Say

Now, there's one problem we need to address. In order to get many of these benefits, you have to actually convey what you're doing for your community. Essentially, you have to include philanthropy within your marketing efforts. You might be able to see the problem here. While I know you're not doing this *just* for the business implication, the general public doesn't necessarily know that—and boy, are there a lot of skeptical people out there.

So how do you communicate this to the public to secure those benefits without virtue signaling? Well, we can start by covering what *not* to say.

The Big Check Photo-Op

We've all seen this before: A business decides it needs to increase its "goodwill" in the community and writes a *big* check (literally and figuratively) to a local nonprofit. This check and the accompanying press release or social post have a short half-life. In the end, this isn't going to provide any meaningful impact on the bottom line of your business. And more importantly, it often doesn't lead to the actual improvement in goodwill you'd hoped for. Don't do this.

"Proud Sponsor"

Putting the words "Proud Sponsor of [insert organization here]" on your website, social media, or blog does not adequately communicate your values. It's overused to the point where it can become meaningless to an audience. I joke with my clients that "sponsors need to stop being so proud!"

While you can (and should) broadcast your sponsorships on your website and in other marketing materials, the lesson here is that just giving a minimum amount per month and slapping the "proud sponsor of" verbiage on your website isn't enough. Being a sponsor is great, but if you want to get true value out of it, it has to be more than just writing a check and adding a logo to your website. Later, we'll cover how to do sponsorships *right*.

Telling People How Much Money You Give

"We give $10,000 per year to [insert organization here]." This form of communication is a double-edged sword. Yes, it may be impressive that you give away a large sum of money, but it can also have a negative impact on your brand.

One issue that arises from this type of communication is that your potential patients may think it's not enough money. "Oh, the dentist who probably drives a Porsche and tows his boat to his lake house every weekend donated a few grand? That's *sooo* kind of him!" It doesn't matter how much money you actually give in relation to your income because the average person won't ever know that. Their perspective will be skewed according to whatever made-up scale they have in their head.

The other issue that arises is when a patient doesn't care past their own pocket: "Don't overcharge me for dentistry so you can give the money to a charity—just give me a discount!" That's certainly a thought that will run through some people's minds. And if you're living paycheck to paycheck, that's reasonable. This is why I don't advise sharing the specific amount of money you donate.

I went through this process with Richard, the traveling dentist who turned practice owner I mentioned previously. He's a veteran, so when it came time to look for a philanthropic effort, he knew he wanted to give back to the veteran community. He found an organization called Quilts of Valor that makes handmade quilts for veterans who are nominated by their community. His first instinct was to say, "For every new patient, we'll donate x dollars," but that didn't sit right with me for all the reasons I've just mentioned. After some discussion, we shifted the messaging: Instead of focusing on money, they now put it in terms of quilts donated. I don't know the specific number off the top of my head, but it's something like, "For every twenty-five patients, we donate a quilt to a veteran to honor their service." This subtle shift transformed the message from one about dollars to one about genuinely giving back to the community. The focus became about the impact—honoring veterans' service—rather than the monetary value of the donation.

What to Do Instead

Now that you know what *not* to say, let's talk about what to do instead. You need to be able to communicate your philanthropy in a way that will result in a positive reaction. The method for doing this is actually incredibly simple. Instead of virtue signaling or calling attention to how much money you give, tell your community about the *impact* your contributions are making.

Let's say you want to give $5,000 per year to a local nonprofit. Ask them what $5,000 does for their beneficiaries. If that helps twenty kids go to summer camp for free, then your message is, "Every year our practice sponsors twenty kids to go to summer camp." To improve that statement, you can add your "why." Discovering your "why" is an important step in determining to whom, and how, you donate.

Volunteering, Nonprofit Partnerships, and Sponsorships

Once you've made the decision to give back in some capacity, you'll want to spend some time on the first part of DRI: *defining* exactly what you want to do. There are many options here, and if you want to do this right, you'll need to think carefully about what makes the most sense for you and your business. This is more than just choosing a charity and writing a check.

I like to break this down into three main buckets: volunteering, nonprofit partnerships, and sponsorships. We've already covered how some of these can be implemented in your marketing strategy, but now we'll dive a bit deeper into how these work so you can understand when and how to use them in your business.

Volunteering

Philanthropy is typically associated with financial giving. There are a few buildings at your alma mater that are there because of philanthropy, and the name on the front proves it. But philanthropy doesn't always need to be monetary. Time and service can be a form of philanthropy. In our practice, we work with a few organizations on an anonymous basis to provide free dental care to women who have been abused or rescued from sex trafficking.

We also take part in community work days. This is one of those activities that checks all the boxes for a positive work environment. It's also a good way to gauge whether your employees are truly aligned with your practice's vision, mission, and core values. If they are, they're probably going to *love* this experience and actively participate in it. If someone is grumbling or making the experience negative for everyone, you'll want to nip that in the bud. Send them home and maybe don't ask them to come back to work. That's a sign you have an employee, not a member of your team.

Sponsorships

A sponsorship is any situation where you're giving dollars in exchange for some level of exposure—whether that's at a one-off physical event or an ongoing sponsorship you might mention on your website and in your marketing. Sponsorships are not a great way to "market" your business and don't always communicate your values well. Why? Because, put simply, it's difficult to find events or organizations to sponsor that have a direct correlation to your dental practice.

Take Red Bull, for example. Red Bull sponsors extreme sporting events, which makes sense because their energy drinks have a direct connection to extreme sports. They also have a scope and scale to their advertising budget that allows for mass media and broad spectrum marketing. Your dental practice probably doesn't have either of those things. There are few organizations or events that have a direct correlation to your dentistry. Sure, you could sponsor a dental expo or an organization that promotes oral health—but your potential patients are not interested in those things. Those are for dentists, and you're not marketing yourself to dentists.

You could argue that sponsoring an organization or event that's highly aligned with your avatar might generate some results, or that having some banners at a local event or your name on the back of a youth sports team may bring some awareness to your practice. But let me ask you this: Have you ever picked a company because of a banner on the back wall of a high school gymnasium? Probably not. And there aren't many people who would.

While you shouldn't expect a direct result from sponsorships, they can sometimes be worth it given their low cost and positive community impact. I like to think of sponsorships more like a billboard—something that isn't going to directly drive patients to your practice but will help with brand recognition over time, making potential patients more likely to choose you when they're searching for a dentist.

The secondary benefit of sponsorship comes from your current patients. When they're at their kid's little league game, and they see your banner, it reminds them that you're aligned with their values and increases the chance they'll talk about you to the families near them. "Oh hey, that's my dentist!" It's a long-term investment in your community presence.

I choose to sponsor not for marketing purposes, but to share my values with the community. It's a donation. It makes me feel good to know I've supported a local 5k for charity or helped the wrestling team rent a bus to go to the state tournament. As long as your expectations are in line with what sponsorships are—a donation—then sponsor away. If you're hoping that a sponsorship will be your next big break and patients will be flowing in, think again. If that's what you're looking for, paid advertising will be a much better use of your time and money.

Nonprofit Partnerships

This is my recommended strategy. There's no better way to get the most out of a philanthropic endeavor than partnering with a nonprofit organization. When done right, this can be an incredibly beneficial experience for everyone involved: you, your practice, the organization, and your community.

Choosing the right partner is incredibly important, and it goes back to your personal vision, mission, and core values. You have to have a personal connection to the nonprofit or their beneficiaries. What do you authentically stand for? What change do you specifically want to see in the world? What hardships have you endured that you'd like to help other people avoid? And what organizations are *actually* generating results in those areas? These are the questions you should be asking yourself when thinking about what type of organization you want to partner with. This is the "why" that will ensure your partnerships are authentically aligned with your practice.

It's tempting to look for a big group with a large social media following because it's flashy, and you think aligning with them will bring you new patients. It won't. I've seen too many dentists go this route: "If I partner with [insert well-known charity here], then I'll gain access to their audience, and more people will hear about my dental office, and I'll get more patients!" This thinking is inauthentic and fails consistently. Without a personal connection to the nonprofit and their beneficiaries, the motivation to work with them fades away, and the endeavor becomes meaningless. Or worse, people see it for what it is—a gimmick—and are turned away from your practice.

Growing up, I was obsessed with dogs. My parents, however, were less inclined toward canines. After several years of harassing, begging, and bargaining, my parents said I could get a dog. *Victory!* There were two conditions: I had to buy it with my own money, *and* I had to pay for the fence it would require. I'm sure they thought that would get me off their back.

So at the age of eleven, I woke up every day at 5:15 a.m. to get to Hodges Blueberry Farm by 6:00 a.m. I picked buckets and buckets of blueberries all summer long. (I didn't eat a single blueberry for almost twenty years after that summer.) During the weekends, I worked at the local shotgun shooting range, where my job was to sit in a concrete bunker, loading clay pigeons on the launchers before they were flung in to the air. I made just enough to buy Jazz, a mutt from the pound, and the materials to build the fence.

My love for dogs didn't go away. During my time running the construction company, I regularly volunteered at a doggy daycare that taught job skills to homeless youth and provided them with a steady income so they could become fully independent. When you're sleeping on the streets, a dog can offer some of the same elements of a home like companionship, warmth, and protection. The homeless community has a strong bond with dogs, and I got to see firsthand how powerful that relationship can be.

All this to say, when it came time to choose a nonprofit to partner with, the answer was obvious. I knew I wanted to partner with a dog-oriented organization. Today, my practice partners with an organization called Paws4People that provides service dogs to individuals and organizations at no charge. We have a strong partnership where I use my own time, money, and community influence to benefit their organization. And let me tell you, it's been one of the most rewarding and enjoyable experiences of my career.

Every year, Paws4People holds their biggest fundraising event, the Puppy Derby, on the same day as the Kentucky Derby. Everyone dresses up in their finest—the ladies are in their fascinators, the guys wear their bow ties, and we all sip mint juleps in true Southern fashion. Throughout the event, there's an entire litter of puppies wearing numbered racing jerseys running around. People can take photos with them, play with them—it's a great time. And then at the end of the event, they put the puppies in the racing start box, and I get the honor of opening the starting gates and releasing the puppies. They race down the track and the whole thing is hysterical—there's always one social butterfly who stops to greet every single person along the way, and usually one that decides to turn around and run back into the starting box. It's legitimately one of my favorite days of the year.

This partnership has opened up incredible opportunities I never would've imagined. Recently, they invited me to be a "shoe guy" at their Wine, Women, & Shoes fundraiser. I got to greet over 400 women at the event, wearing my favorite fancy shoes, and I even did a runway walk wearing $4,000 of high-end men's fashion. The whole thing was a blast, but it was also an incredible opportunity to connect with hundreds of potential patients who share my values. That crowd was almost entirely made up of middle- to upper-class women who love dogs—my exact avatar. You simply can't buy that kind of authentic connection and exposure as a dentist.

Through these events, I've also built relationships with local news anchors, business journals, and Chamber of Commerce leaders—all because we share common values around helping others. It has nothing to do with crown pricing or insurance networks. This partnership has been transformative both personally and professionally. The community impact continues to grow, and I've gained lifelong patients who feel like family because we bonded over our shared love of dogs.

I encourage you to find out what makes you tick—what experiences you've had, passions you want to rekindle, or groups in need that call to you. Take that authentic desire to narrow your search and find the organization that best fits that authenticity. Reach out and ask how you can best serve them. When you find the right partnership, you won't regret it—in fact, you might just find a new favorite activity!

The Final Piece of the Puzzle

All these philanthropic endeavors might sound great, but don't feel pressured to implement them right away. When I first started working with Richard, for example, the idea of charitable giving wasn't even on the table. We prioritized the fundamentals first to ensure his practice was not only profitable, but that his time and energy were protected. Once things stabilized, we then looked into philanthropy, and he found the Quilts of Valor organization.

There's a reason I left this chapter for the end. This is really what we've been building toward. The leadership principles in part I, the management systems in part II, and the marketing strategies in part III are all designed to help you build a practice that serves you first. Because once your practice is truly serving you, you can start focusing on serving others in meaningful ways. Your dental practice becomes more than just a business—it becomes a vehicle for positive change in your community.

This is the final piece of the puzzle, and it's worth being patient to get here. You first need that solid foundation. But as you work on the fundamentals, keep this end goal in sight. Every system you create, every team member you develop, every marketing campaign you launch—they're all steps toward building something bigger than yourself. A practice that not only generates seven figures, but also makes a real difference in people's lives.

That's the true power of being a healthcare entrepreneur. You have the unique opportunity to build a business that enriches your life, empowers your team, serves your patients, and uplifts your community. When you get there—and you will get there—you'll find it's the most fulfilling part of practice ownership.

Define, Refine, Implement

Define: Determine what you want to accomplish through philanthropy, and why you want to do this.

Refine: Research and identify what you're looking for in a partnership that will help you accomplish that.

Implement: Partner with an organization that is aligned with your vision, mission, and core values.

CONCLUSION

Everything we've covered in this book—every system, strategy, and framework—serves one purpose: to help you create a practice that fulfills the life you want to live. Not just someday, but every single day.

Your practice can and should be an engine for your ideal life. When you operate with intention—when every action is aligned with your vision—your practice becomes a source of energy rather than a drain on it. You can enjoy your work, knowing that each day is building toward something meaningful—not just for you, but for your team, your patients, and your community.

I won't sugarcoat it—this journey requires intense focus, unwavering effort, and the courage to step outside your comfort zone. You'll have to make tough decisions. You'll have to change deeply ingrained habits. You'll have to do the hard work.

Yet consider the alternative: continuing to live a life that doesn't fulfill you. Spending years—maybe decades—doing things you don't enjoy, working in ways that drain you, and missing moments with your family that you can never get back. That path might seem easier because it's familiar, but in reality, it's far more difficult. It's the slow erosion of your dreams, one compromised day at a time.

Remember our order of operations. You can't build a dream house without first visualizing it and making the architectural plans. Start by defining your vision—the life you truly want to live. Build the foundation through your mission and core values, creating a filter that supports every future decision. Frame the structure through leadership that inspires and empowers your team. Install the systems that create consistency and freedom. And design your marketing to authentically attract the right patients.

This progression isn't random; it's your blueprint for success. Each element builds upon the last, creating a practice that is both profitable and fulfilling—not just for you, but for your team, your patients, and your community. When your practice truly serves you, you gain the freedom to serve others in meaningful ways. That's why we ended with philanthropy. It's the ultimate expression of a practice that's working the way it should.

So now it's your turn. The blueprint is in your hands. If you're feeling overwhelmed, remember that you don't have to implement everything at once (nor should you). Start with your vision and take small, intentional steps forward. Every lifestyle choice, every system you create, every team member you develop, every marketing campaign you launch are all steps toward building something bigger than yourself. A practice that not only generates seven figures but also makes a real difference in people's lives.

And by the way, you're not alone on this journey. If you need additional support, visit drbenfriberg.com/bookresources—all the templates and resources I've mentioned in this book are designed to make your life easier, so I'd encourage you to use them. You can also reach out to me directly through the website—I'd love to hear from you! Whether you have questions about implementing these concepts, you've had a breakthrough moment, or you just want to share how this book has impacted your practice, send me an email. Nothing brings me more joy than hearing success stories from dentists who are building practices that truly fulfill them.

Finally, if you're looking for a community of like-minded people, I invite you to join the Thrive Collective—our community of dentists who are committed to practicing differently, who refuse to accept the status quo, and who believe that dentistry can be both profitable and fulfilling. If you've made it this far, I know you'll be a great fit.

Thank you for taking this journey with me. By reading this book, you've already taken the first step toward transformation. Now it's time for action. Because every day that you operate your practice with intention—every day that you make decisions aligned with your vision—you're not just building a better business, you're building a better life.

The best time to start is now. Here's to creating a practice that fulfills the life you want to live, one intentional day at a time.

ENDNOTES

[i] Colin R. Gagg, "Cement and Concrete as an Engineering Material: An Historic Appraisal and Case Study Analysis," *Engineering Failure Analysis* 40 (2014): 114–140, https://www.sciencedirect.com/science/article/abs/pii/S1350630714000387

[ii] Ian Coss, host, *The Big Dig*, podcast, episode 8, "I Want Justice for What Happened," WGBH, November 8, 2023, https://www.wgbh.org/podcasts/the-big-dig/part-8-i-want-justice-for-what-happened.

[iii] "Dentist Workforce FAQs," American Dental Association, https://www.ada.org/resources/research/health-policy-institute/dentist-workforce

[iv] Myriah Shimatsu, "Nobody Likes a Pain in the Neck," *Journal of the Colorado Dental Association* Fall (2019), https://cdaonline.org/news/latest-news/nobody-likes-a-pain-in-the-neck/

[v] SpaceX, https://www.spacex.com/.

[vi] "About," Microsoft, https://www.microsoft.com/en-us/about.

[vii] Amy Gallo, "What Is Psychological Safety?" *Harvard Business Review*, February 15, 2023, https://hbr.org/2023/02/what-is-psychological-safety.

[viii] Jacob Morgan, "The Top 10 Factors for On-the-Job Employee Happiness," *Forbes*, updated December 10, 2021, https://www.forbes.com/sites/jacobmorgan/2014/12/15/the-top-10-factors-for-on-the-job-employee-happiness/.

[ix] Liangcan Liu, Zhitao Wan, and Li Wang, "Cross-Level Research on the Impact of Self-Serving Leadership on Employee Innovation Behavior: The Roles of Workplace Anxiety and Team Psychological Safety," *Frontiers in Psychology* 13 (2022), https://www.frontiersin.org/journals/psychology/articles/10.3389/fpsyg.2022.1069022/full?form=MG0AV3.

[x] "Diffusion of Responsibility," Wikipedia, https://en.wikipedia.org/wiki/Diffusion_of_responsibility.

ACKNOWLEDGMENTS

This book would not have been possible without the support, guidance, and inspiration of so many incredible people.

To Jayme Amos, Stephen Trutter, and Stacey Peters at Ideal Practices—thank you for being with me every step of the way during my journey through practice ownership. Your expertise and encouragement have been invaluable.

To Dan Green, Jay Reid, and Michael Profant—my first business mentors over two decades ago—you laid the foundation for my understanding of leadership and entrepreneurship. Your lessons continue to resonate with me today.

To Bill Blatchford, Christina Blatchford, and Keri Weron—your mentorship unlocked a belief in myself that I didn't know I was capable of. I am forever grateful for your insights and support.

To my parents—your unwavering support and encouragement have been the bedrock of my success. Thank you for always being my greatest cheerleaders.

And to Ella, my wife—the best tour guide on our journey through life—your love, wisdom, and partnership mean the world to me. Thank you for sharing this incredible adventure with me.

This book is a reflection of all the lessons, inspiration, and love I have received from each of you. Thank you for being a part of my story.

www.ingramcontent.com/pod-product-compliance
Lightning Source LLC
Chambersburg PA
CBHW020455030426
42337CB00011B/124